End Homelessness Now!

The Road to A Solution

The Home GAP Initiative

Written By

J. M. Montgomery
Author
First Published Works - 2020

Homelessness is a Worldwide Problem.
Let's Fix It So It Will Never Happen To Anyone Anymore.

Ordering Information:
Book Title: End Homelessness Now! – The Road to A Solution
Please visit: http://end-homelessness-now.com
For details, contact jmichaelmontgomery@end-homelessness-now.com

Print ISBN: 978-1-7351324—3-3

$39.95

ISBN 978-1-7351324-3-3

53995>

9 781735 132433

Printed in the United States of America.

First Edition

Cover Design by:
Marijke van Leeuwen
www.HummingbirdBookCovers.com

Co-Editor:
Patrick Robinson

Author's Pledge

5% of Author's Profits will be Donated to "Operation Sacred Trust" in Miami, Fl - Veterans Administration Supportive Services for Veteran Families program.

For more information on "Operation Sacred Trust"
Just look on the next page →

Figure 1, Turner, J. (Logo Courtesy of Operation Sacred Trust, 2020).

"*Purpose Built Families Foundation's* Operation Sacred Trust (OST, 2020)[1] collaboration *is a nationally accredited, public-private partnership for homelessness prevention and rapid rehousing. Fundamental to the approach of* OST *is attention to factors that create, contribute to, and address problems in living as reflected by challenges to housing stability for low-income Veteran families.*

The Operation Sacred Trust ("OST") *Program is charged with bringing unique approaches, experiences, and expertise to serve homeless and low-income Veterans in Miami-Dade and Broward counties, located in the heart of South Florida. These counties have been hit particularly hard by the economic downturn, as evidenced by the high level of poverty, low median income, and skyrocketing foreclosure rates. Veterans have been particularly affected, with over 1,000 homeless Veterans and over 20,000 low-income Veterans living in the service area.* Operation Sacred Trust *is unique in that it combines proven traditional outreach and case management best practices with novel nontraditional service delivery methods. Funding for this initiative has been awarded by the Veterans Administration Supportive Services for Veteran Families program."*

---

[1] Operation Sacred Trust, Veterans Administration Supportive Services for Veteran Families Program. www.411veterans.com

Dedication

I dedicate this book first and foremost to my mother, Linda Montgomery; she passed away on January 18, 2017. Her cancer did not deter her from keeping me focused on finishing my academic endeavors. I will always miss her. I also want to thank my father, James Montgomery, for fifty-seven years, he has been my pillar and inspiration. He has taught me patience and motivation. I also wish to thank my brother Stephen; he has always been helpful when I needed it the most.

– "My heart will always thank all three of you."

To my best friend and soulmate, Miraflor and your daughter Ara. Although you live halfway around the world, you are an inspiration, and you both have been a supporting rock in my life. I am very appreciative of what you have gone through in your experiences. For you to support me through my life's challenges speaks volumes as to your character, which is my tower of strength.

– "I thank you both from the bottom of my heart."

J. Michael Montgomery

Loving Son, Brother, and Best Friend.

Figure 2. Montgomery, M. (Photographer) (2020, May 26).
Montgomery Family Crest.

Acknowledgments

To more than the forty professors at Florida International University (FIU), **"GO PANTHERS,"** that have educated me over the last four years, - I express my thanks to all of you. You actively played a part in furthering my education to get me to this point; I appreciate you passing your knowledge onto me. Your support and encouraging words as professors will stay with me for many years to come.

– "Thank you."

J. Michael Montgomery
Master of Public Administration
Florida International University

Pi Alpha Alpha

Honor Society[2]

Figure 3. Merille, E. (Photographer).(Circa 2019, Jan).
Florida International University Panther Statue.
Retrieved from https://www.flickr.com/photos/fiu/8489551367

---

[2] Π A A – The Global Honor Society for Public Affairs & Administration. Retrieved from http://pialphaalpha.org (2020).

Preface

End Homelessness Now! – The Road to A Solution

The Home Giveaway Program Initiative

This work discusses several solutions to reduce those issues associated with chronic homelessness in the United States and possibly for the rest of the world. One such solution is a theoretical program [3] that the author designed is called "The Home Giveaway Program Initiative" (Home Gap). This research will discuss other practical approaches to be implemented along with this proposed pilot homeless home giveaway program.

The research conducted in this book is to assess the various costs and alternatives for providing long-term solutions to the identifiable issues of chronic homelessness. More particularly, this work focuses on the role played by participating banks in which donating homes to any government agency would be conducive to reducing the chronic homelessness numbers for any given society. These homes are necessary to help the homeless population, thus making them active and productive citizens, thus increasing the gross domestic product (GDP) for any community that is taking care of the homeless.

In Montgomery's (2019) research, in the future, The City of Miami-Dade will be presented with three project proposals as a Policy Brief, discussing these plans as viable options for a future policy change to aid in reducing the issues associated with the homeless population in this district.

Project 1 proposal is that the do-nothing approach is merely maintaining the status quo to aid the homeless population with temporary aid or shelter. The status quo is costing the county $44,678,282 annually in taking care of the homeless in Miami-Dade (Montgomery, 2019).

Project 2 proposal would be to model the Kansas City, Missouri "Tiny Homes Project" (2018). This program has been built for veterans transitioning out of homelessness. If this project is implemented, Miami-Dade would need to build 3,839 single one-room 166 square foot homes [4] with kitchen, bathroom, and amenities for the homeless in Miami-Dade (Home Advisor, 2019).

Project 2 would cost the county an additional $25,000 per home that is built on donated land— adding $95,975,000 to the county's budget of $44,678,282 per year that the county is already spending on the homeless state of affairs. According to Cunningham & Batko (2018),[5] it will be crucial to allow authorized contractors to construct affordable homes. Just as Kansas City, Missouri, organized in building homes strictly for the veteran community.[6]

---

[3] Copyright Statement - From "Reducing Homelessness in Miami-Dade County," by J. Michael Montgomery: Unpublished manuscript from Florida International University. Copyright 2019. Adapted with permission.
[4] Home Advisor. "How Much Does It Cost To Build A House?" (2019).
[5] M. Cunningham & S. Batko. "Rapid Re-housing's Role in Responding to Homelessness." *Metropolitan Housing.* (2018).
[6] Village of Tiny Homes Built for Homeless Veterans In Kansas City. (2018).

Miami-Dade would have the same option of either taking no action or constructing small houses for homeless people or homeless veterans regardless of discharge status. Just as the Veterans Community Project in Kansas City, Missouri, achieved. This Kansas City, Missouri Community Project was established in 2015.

Figures 4 and 5. *(Kantor, W. 2018). Veterans Community Project's village. Retrieved from* https://people.com/human-interest/hero-group-veterans-community-project-tiny-homes/

Project 3 proposal has the lowest net present value and would be the best choice - Maximizing on benefits of effectiveness, efficiency, and equity for Miami-Dade County.

Miami-Dade would start seeing property rental revenues generated from those homeless individuals participating in The Home Giveaway Program Initiative starting in the third year after the implementation of the plan. After the tenth year, the county would then see property tax revenues increasing after that. The qualified homeless individual would participate in specific programs that would meet their long-term personal needs - this includes such as taking care of their medical issues, mental health concerns, and reestablishing themselves into the workforce.

With Project 3, Miami-Dade would start seeing a reduction in county expenditures after the tenth year. The county would then see a reduction in the current budget of $44,678,282, starting in the eleventh year (see the Cost-Benefit Analysis Data Sheet in Appendix A**).**

Miami-Dade would be spending respectively $44,678,282 in year eleven, $35,742,625.60 in year twelve, $26,806,969.20 in year thirteen, $17,871,312.80 in year fourteen, $8,935,656.40 in year fifteen, and little costs in the sixteenth year and after that. Project 3 was the most effective way as it had the highest Net Present Value (NPV).

Chart 01 – Criteria for Evaluating Alternatives

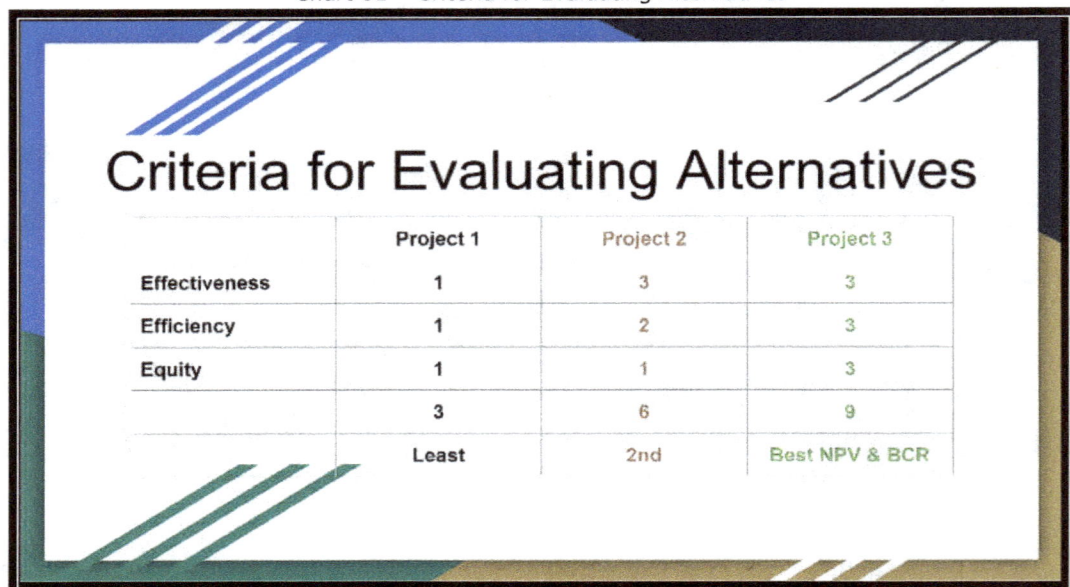

Evaluating Alternatives (Montgomery, 2019). [7]

Project 3 would be the best economical method of assessing the best value of innovative performance measures for this type of project, utilizing "The Home Giveaway Program Initiative."

This book bases its argument that "The Home Giveaway Program Initiative" provides the best approach for mitigating the issues of chronic homelessness by any government agency in the US and abroad. Supplemental alternatives are discussed as part of the undertaking on the homelessness issue. Secondary data was used to support the main argument raised in this research for future review by the Miami-Dade government in the implementation of The Home Giveaway Program Initiative.

Table of Contents

List for Charts

List of Abbreviations and Acronyms

AMI	Area Median Income
ASPE	Assistant Secretary for Planning and Evaluation
BCR	Benefit-Cost Ratio
CBA	Cost-Benefit Analysis
CFR	Code of Federal Regulations
GDP	Gross Domestic Product
Home GAP	Home Giveaway Program
HPRP	Homelessness Prevention and Rapid Re-Housing Program
HUD	Housing and Urban Development
HUD-Vash	Housing & Urban Development VA Supportive Housing Program
IBRD	International Bank for Reconstruction and Development
IDA	International Development Association
ITS	Interrupted Time Series Design
J2SI	Journey to Social Inclusion
LCSW	Licensed Clinical Social Worker
LIHTC	Low Income Housing Tax Credit
MRM	Miami Rescue Mission
MSW	Master of Social Work
NPV	Net Present Value
PAAVO	The National Programme to End Long-term Homelessness
PIT	Point-in-Time
PTSD	Post-Traumatic Stress Disorder
VA	Veteran's Administration
VHA	Veteran's Health Administration

Foreword

Homelessness has been a great challenge affecting many people around the world. The issue of homelessness often gets ignored because it looks familiar to many people. On the streets of our world, homeless individuals and families are living under impoverished conditions. Now with the rise of COVID-19 has disrupted many lives. Many have lost their jobs during this crisis. More are now experiencing homelessness for the first time and thus exacerbating the problem that is existing already. The issue is less addressed; in enforcing laws, many nations show fewer concerns to homeless families. There are no adequate plans to give the homeless families better lives, the issue gets often ignored, and the victims continue to pay the price. This book proposes a long-term ten-year program that can help all stakeholders dealing with the issues of homelessness. Those participants that would benefit will be the homeless individuals, any stakeholders such as social workers, business owners, banks, and lastly, all government agencies, and officials.

During this time in the history of dealing with COVID-19, homeless individuals and families are at high risk of contracting and spreading the infection; that is why they need proper attention. Homeless people live under impoverished conditions in congregate settings. They mostly live in abandoned settings such as old buildings or in open areas, and this risks transmission of many diseases. These individuals cannot access essential hygiene services such as soap and water that are needed to stop the spread of communicable diseases. Many people living in the streets have chronic mental and physical conditions, and they cannot access medical centers easily.

These psychiatric conditions could aggravate feelings of hopelessness following the unavailability of elective and non-emergency psychiatric services in strained public health systems, potentially increasing the risk of erratic behavior that could put this vulnerable population at risk during the COVID-19 outbreak (Tsai & Wilson, 2020). Homeless families are the most vulnerable groups as the epidemic continues to be a public safety issue. Therefore, it is essential to devise some mechanisms to deal with the issue of homelessness permanently.

This book proposes a long-term ten-year program to cushion the blow of most identifiable issues of homelessness. States all over the world should put some financial resources aside to help those vulnerable individuals and families living in a homeless state. Unlike those citizens who have financial stability, the homeless person needs special attention. They should feel like part of the society in which they live, and the best way to make them feel so is extending a helping hand during these challenging times. Governments, businesses, and other philanthropists must give back to society through a definitive long-term plan.

Once homeless individuals are given an avenue never to become homeless again, then they can contribute significantly to the Gross Domestic Product (GDP) for the community for which they live. After all, isn't it the goal of enlightened civilizations to have a well self-supporting society? It would be morally unethical to assume that a homeless individual or family can reinject themselves into the working class without the assistance of the community in which they live due to the lack of unavailable resources.

The best way to deal with the issue of homeless individuals and families currently is to offer them safe places where they can call home. These individuals and families should be tested and given regular medical attention to keep them safe. These individuals and families need clean water and adequate food supply to keep them healthy during the epidemic. However, this is just for the short term; the long-term ten year-program proposed in this book can help deal with the issues of chronic homelessness and enhance sustainability and become a valued asset to the working class and local communities.

Making any long-term ten-year homeless program realistic should focus on already existing homes. These existing homes are classified as "Non-Income Producing Assets" that are owned by banks or other financial institutions. These assets are the focal point of "The Home GAP Initiative" that will be discussed in this book.

The target should be to rehabilitate as many homeless individuals and families as possible; these people need places to call home. States should focus on educating homeless individuals to equip them with the knowledge to turn things around. Homeless individuals have many potentials, only that they do not have the right platforms to unlock what they have within themselves. All stakeholders need to work collectively to address the issues of homelessness. The homeless, social workers, philanthropists, and all governments need to come together to devise long-term solutions, and The Home GAP Initiative discussed in this book aims to address all these critical areas.

"As long as greed is stronger than compassion,

there will always be suffering."

Rusty Eric – Author[8].

---

[8] From "The Fighter Within" - by Rusty Eric Author. (n.d.)

Introduction

0.00   Statement of the Problem

Long-Term Vs. Short-Term Solutions to Homelessness [9]

   The issue concerning homelessness is one that requires immediate attention to long-term solutions since it improves the livelihood of a multitude of people. Three thousand eight hundred thirty-nine homeless individuals in Miami-Dade cost the county approximately $44.68 million annually to make available essential services (Ullman, 2016). The results from a 2016 NHIP report on homelessness in Florida found that money for 2,881 vouchers for permanent house units across the counties of Florida would require $34.2 million annually to ensure case management, project administration, and development of rental subsidies.

   As unsheltered homelessness decreases, homelessness in the County of Miami-Dade should remain at a downward trend as well. Through affordable housing, this is likely to ensure a proper balance between the two as well as promoting a long-term solution to homelessness (Ullman, 2016). A decrease in homelessness would mean that individuals would have better standards of living, equally leading to the growth of other aspects of the community, such as healthcare.

   According to a 2019 census study, the trends indicate that more individuals encountering homelessness are likely to move off the streets of Miami-Dade, which will be the case if the homeless individuals are given access to accessible and affordable housing as it is fundamental to maintain sustainability. Whereas the populace of sheltered homeless persons in Miami-Dade County appreciated by 5% from 2018-2019, those individuals that were homeless in the community decreased by 2% as per the data collected by Miami-Dade County (Homeless Trust, 2019).

---

[9] Copyright Statement -   From "Reducing Homelessness in Miami-Dade County," by J. Michael Montgomery: Unpublished manuscript from Florida International University. Copyright 2019. Adapted with permission.

Previously, programs have been developed to address homelessness; however, since they have only been short-term, minimal success has been realized. Most of the solutions to homelessness have been delivered in a general approach, which should not be the case. In consideration of the causes of homelessness, it manifests through cultural, language, social, and economic differences between individuals both in Miami-Dade County and other communities worldwide. When short-terms solutions are developed to address homelessness, various issues could be left unaddressed, such as root-causes, which leads to a predisposition to chronic homelessness. As such, it is outright that short-term solutions could only address homelessness in acute cases since there is no single solution for all.

According to Homeless Trust (2019), approximately 3,839 people in Miami-Dade County are homeless even though the homeless population has been on a slowly decreasing trend. It is essential to note that some of the significant constraints minimal to homeless people attributed to issues such as unemployment and poverty, immigration, mental or health conditions, substance abuse, relationship breakdowns, lack of affordable housing, abusive homes, among other personal issues. It is noted that health-related issues associated with the onset of the COVID-19 pandemic are now exacerbating the issues of homelessness.

Today, compared to other continuums in Florida, the displaced population in Miami-Dade County is low. However, the primary issue surrounding homelessness needs a long-term solution to ensure that the problem is tackled to deliver real change with a positive impact on the social, economic, cultural, and other community elements. Eradicating homelessness will ultimately increase the number of tax-paying citizens, and the resultant increase in GDP would benefit everyone in the county (Montgomery, 2019). Through the "Home Giveaway Program Initiative (Home GAP)," it would ensure that easier access to housing can be offered. Home GAP would deliver significant inroads by providing permanent housing options and a specific focus on the unsheltered individuals. By far, affordable housing is an essential issue to administer long-lasting and real change to the primary issues of homelessness.

Chapter 1

1.01   The Home Giveaway Program Initiative

The Home Giveaway Program[10] Initiative is a theoretical long-term ten-year homeless program that is designed to aid in ending the issues for those individuals whose defined classification status as being "homeless." The author has focused on Miami-Dade County, Florida, as the center of this analysis. Miami-Dade County has a population of 3,839 homeless people (Ullman, 2017)[11], either living on the streets or who are in homeless shelters in the immediate area. Miami-Dade is spending $44,678,282.00 a year to provide for the basic needs of homeless individuals (see the Cost-Benefit Analysis Data Sheet in Appendix A).

The Home GAP Initiative (Montgomery, 2019), is a social project with various stakeholders and community members involved who want to make changes to homeless people's lives. To make them active and productive, tax-paying citizens capable of adding to the GDP for all stakeholders in any governmental jurisdictions who are taking care of the homeless. There are no prior evaluations for this long-term theoretical program. At this current time, there are no active, long-term ten-year programs in the United States that the author is aware of that actively seek to counteract the chronic issues that plague most homeless individuals.

1.02   Extreme Poverty Defined

Persons living in extreme poverty has risen over the years. Measurements of extreme poverty are described by The World Bank (2016)[12] as:

> "It is extremely difficult to measure poverty in a rigorous way, and every country sets its own standards for what is necessary for basic living. There are climate variations: what a person needs to survive in Central Asia for caloric intake, clothing, shelter, and heat is different from what is needed in a tropical location. And the standards vary with development. Richer countries will set a higher standard for what counts as poverty."

> "At the World Bank, we take the information on basic needs collected from the 15 poorest countries and then we average them. That comes out to be about $1.90 per day per person, and that is what we call the global extreme poverty line."

---

[10] Copyright Statement -   From "Reducing Homelessness in Miami-Dade County," by J. Michael Montgomery: Unpublished manuscript from Florida International University. Copyright 2019. Adapted with permission.
[11] Ullman. "STATE OF FLORIDA REPORT: 2016 Homeless Census Estimates and Funding Need to End Chronic Homelessness.
[12] The World Bank. Ending Extreme Poverty. IBRD-IDA. (2016).

"We can monetize a lot of the aspects of poverty—access to clean water and access to health care, for example, are put in monetary terms in our model—but there is a legitimate debate about the multidimensional aspects of poverty. When you talk to the poor, they will talk about a sense of dignity and about having a job, not just receiving money. How do you monetize that? You can monetize access to schooling, but it is more difficult to monetize the quality of schooling. And so on."

1.03   Homeless Data in the United States

A sizable number of American citizens are living under the poverty line (ASPE, 2019)[13]. The homeless problem is persistently getting worse in the United States. The majority of unfortunate people face the challenge of paying for affordable housing, rent, buying food, access to health care, childcare, and education. Decisions are tough when there are inadequate resources to fulfill only some of the requirements. In 2000, approximately 11.3% of the people in the US lived under poverty. Research done by The National Homeless Information Project stated that approximately 3,839 individuals residing in the Miami-Dade area are homeless (Homeless Trust, 2019).

According to the Miami Herald (Gross, 2019) news article dated August 08, stated:

> *"Using data recorded by the US Census Bureau, online loan marketplace LendingTree found earlier this year **that 17.09% of Miami's 2 million households were vacant**. Vacancies include housing that is for seasonal use, for sale, for rent, or unoccupied."*

In the United States, the number of empty homes outnumbers the total of homeless individuals by 6 to 1 (MintPress News Desk, 2015). With 600,000 people in America experiencing homelessness every night (Covert, 2013) [14], there are about 38,000 veterans who are experiencing homelessness. The 6 to 1 ratio applied to the 600,000 homeless individuals living on the streets every night; means 3,600,000 vacant homes in the United States are not generating a revenue stream for the current owners of those units. The owners of these empty or abandoned homes are usually owned by a bank or a financial institution. These unoccupied units are defined as a "Non-Income Producing Asset"[15] as per the Code of Federal Regulations (n.d.).

Advocating for change in how we should take care of our homeless individuals in the United States and worldwide should be the main priority. How we view abandoned properties is essential to conquering this increasing issue of chronic homelessness. For banks and lending institutions to give away homes to such programs as the hypothetical program with "The Home GAP Initiative"[16] makes good business sense. Especially for those who are homeless, the local government, local business owners, the local communities, and any stakeholders who have a conferred interest with this topic.

---

[13] ASPE. "Poverty Guidelines." (2019).

[14] S. Cundiff. Veterans & Addiction: Homelessness & Post-Traumatic Stress Disorder. (2015).

[15] Definition of Value of Non-Income Producing Assets. *Lawinsider.com* (n.d.).

[16] Copyright Statement - From "Reducing Homelessness in Miami-Dade County," by J. Michael Montgomery: Unpublished manuscript from Florida International University. Copyright 2019. Adapted with permission.

Obtaining accurate statistics of homeless people globally can be challenging for assorted reasons. Trying to understand the meaning of the term homeless and homelessness can attract multiple definitions. Such meanings as the absenteeism of acceptable accommodation to the permanent lack of residence provide adequate security that comforts an individual's state of well-being (Padgett, Henwood, & Tsemberis, 2016).

Definitions will vary across all nations. Because homelessness is defined based on the cultural and on established concepts, such as security of ownership and how adequate housing is determined by those governing agencies: Most governments face the challenges of committing to addressing the homelessness issue and having issues of inadequate resources to measure the extent of homelessness. Being considered homeless is embarrassing for the government as well as those individuals who see themselves in this predicament. Also, some parents, some men, but mostly women, do not wish to be regarded as homeless for fear of losing their children to Child Protective Services. Equally painful for some homeless individuals are the adult child who is taking care of an elderly parent who finds themselves in a destitute situation.

Family homelessness is a major social problem that has affected a respectable number of families internationally. It manifests itself through diverse social, cultural, economic, and language contexts globally. Canada also faces a growing rise in the total number of homeless families and is growing in attention per press and media outlets (McElroy, 2019). Many homeless families are dependent on emergency accommodations. The increase in unemployment, the lack of dependable, affordable housing, becoming sick, the many diverse social and economic issues; are becoming policy concerns to every stakeholder on the matter of dealing with homelessness on the whole.

1.04   A Possible Long-Term Solution 17

"The Home Giveaway Program Initiative (Home GAP)," as explained previously, is a new theoretical long-term program concept that has a public evaluation designed by Alvarez & Montgomery, (2019). This program is designed to afford all homeless individuals to make changes in their lives, and when accepted into the Home GAP Initiative can be given a chance in the future to own a home. This home would be gifted to the homeless individual upon completion of this unique program. The homeless individual would agree to participate in a ten-year educational process in which an assigned social worker would layout a treatment plan specific to the homeless person's needs. If this program is approved for implementation by any state facility, they will gift a home to a homeless person upon completion of The Home GAP, a process that will take a minimum of ten years to complete (Montgomery, 2019).

1.05   Providing a Long-Term Solution

Providing homeless services with long-term solutions/goals is the best approach. In an Australian pilot program called the Journey to Social Inclusion (J2SI)[18] showed that building trust with homeless clients proved successful during this short-term study (Johnson, Parkinson, Tseng, & Kuehnle, 2019). J2SI proved that with homeless clients through adequate engagements with therapists and supportive housing agents, it leads to personal growth and a willingness to change for the better.

Madeleine Thiele-Evans with Sacred Heart Mission (Anonymous, 2019)[19] discussed the holistic approach of supportive programs with "Social Inclusion" helps to break the cycle of homelessness.

> *"I have seen this program support people to secure housing and make some great life changes," Madeleine says.*

> *"By building trust with people over time, we as case managers are in a far better place to help people reconnect with their community and develop life skills, meaning they can spread their wings and fly when they are no longer in the program.*

> *"It's important to understand simple tasks we take for granted - like the ability to pay bills or have a shower in the morning - don't necessarily come easy to someone who has experienced long-term homelessness." (Sacred Heart Mission, 2019).*

Implementing the Home GAP Initiative by providing a formal approach for practitioners in re-educating adults (Moran, 1997)[20] who find themselves in a homeless situation better focuses the client on achieving the intended long-term goal of avoiding homelessness in the future.

---

[18] Johnson, G. Long-Term Homelessness: Understanding the Challenge – 12 Months Outcomes From the Journey to Social Inclusion Pilot Program. *SSRN, Elsevier* (2019).
[19] Anonymous. Why our program Journey to Social Inclusion (J2SI) really works. *Sacred Heart Mission* (2019).
[20] Moran, Joseph. Assessing Adult Learning. A Guide for Practitioners. Professional Practices in Adult Education and Human Resource Development Series. *Krieger Publishing Co (1997)*.

1.06   Cost-Effectiveness 21

The Home GAP Initiative is designed not to increase the amount spent by the government on dealing with those homeless individuals. Maintaining current cost levels and implementing the Home GAP Initiative can be achieved by reallocating current resources and personnel into the infrastructure of The Home GAP Initiative project. The program cost for 20 years will not result in additional expenditures to be made except for the starting point. At the beginning of the program, spending more money is expected. Over time, as the program's clients succeed in each of the phases of the program. An increase in revenues comes by paying rent, and the transition to property tax payments after the title is given to the recipient. The government's revenue in property taxes and charges for services will increase for every client who has graduated from the Home GAP Initiative project. The government will now be collecting revenue from non-income producing homes. By implementing the Home GAP Initiative, the government's outstanding debt will eventually reach a breakeven point as to the issue with the costs of taking care of homeless individuals. These expenditures will drastically decrease, and the government's budget can result in higher direct funding.

1.07   Evaluation Design for the Home GAP Initiative

The chosen design for the Home GAP is the Interrupted Time-Series Design (ITS). The ITS is a model to measure the program's results. By analyzing pre-intervention and post-intervention measures (Hatry, Newcomer, Wholey, 2015). The Home GAP Initiative, because it is a long-term, ten-year plan for any government agency and the homeless, will be beneficial to all stakeholders involved. In the beginning, since the Home GAP Initiative is a long-term program, the measurements from the initial start will be set in four stages.

Interventions Stage 1 - The Input Stage will be graded at the end of year two. This section includes Part one – Inputs, Part two – Activities, and Part three – Outputs. (See Page 34).

Interventions Stage 2 – The Short-Term Outcome Stage will be graded at the end of year four. (See Page 38).

Interventions Stage 3 – The Intermediate Outcome Stage to be graded at the end of year seven. (See Page 39).

Intervention Stage 4 – The Long-Term Outcome Stage will be graded at the end of year ten. (See Page 40).

Interventions for the Home GAP Initiative will start two years after the program begins accepting homeless clients into the program. A total of ten years is accounted for all four stages of the Home GAP Initiative listed above. After the tenth year, the program shall be monitored on a biannual basis.

Future growth of The Home GAP Initiative is expected. "When the word gets out," other homeless individuals will migrate to cities offering The Home GAP Initiative from different parts of the United States, even from other parts of the world. Therefore, the evaluation plan will be an ongoing process to continually measure how effective "The Home GAP Initiative" will be to house homeless people in this long-term ten-year program.

In Phase Three, though not an intervention, but part of the program, it is expected that there will be some individuals who will have a problem with participation during any stage of the Home GAP Initiative. Those individuals on a case-by-case basis who are identified by a Masters in Social Work (MSW) will be reprocessed back to Stage One, Part two. Also expected are individuals who will refuse to participate for any reason and will be dismissed from the Home GAP Initiative. These individuals will be admitted to a local temporary shelter for entry into a transitional housing program. Those individuals refusing or who cannot comply with their treatment plan a second time are moved to Phase Three. It is the goal of the Home GAP Initiative, knowing that there will be those individuals who will not make it through completion that their housing issue will still be taken care of on a humanitarian level.

In the evaluation design, two graphs presented measure three primary goals of the program; the reduction of government expenditures over time, the number of individuals recruited into the program, and is contrasted by those who are no longer eligible to participate in the program (See Measurement Indicators. (See Charts 6 and 7**).**

The Home GAP Initiative is a theoretical program, and the Interrupted Time-Series (ITS) [22] is the most efficient design to compare the data set of these measures. While other housing programs are short-term, the design exemplifies that the program is leading the intended outcome of reducing homelessness over this long-term ten-year plan. It also separates other alternatives as to why homelessness is decreasing, making the architecture of the design internally valid. It is proficient in external validity, as this design can be generalized to other sectors in the United States and Worldwide for people who are facing an analogous situation. Lastly, each intervention accounts for the same number of individuals who started in the program (or who are dismissed) are accounted for after each stage of this developed program.

The Home GAP Initiative will have no additional out-of-pocket expenses for taxpayers in Miami-Dade. The program is designed and intended to utilize the county's infrastructure that is already in place – diverting the $44,678,282.00 a year towards The Home GAP Initiative and the professionals that the county is already using, such as social workers or other county employees. These people would be predesignated by the mayor and his implementation of management teams that are already on the county's payroll to see that all phases of the Home GAP are adequately addressed.

---

[22] Copyright Statement - From "Public Evaluation Design for Miami-Dade Home GAP," by J. Michael Montgomery and Sandro Alvarez, 2019: Unpublished manuscript. *Florida International University.* Adapted with permission.

1.08   Logic Model Stages 1. 2, 3, & 4 [23]

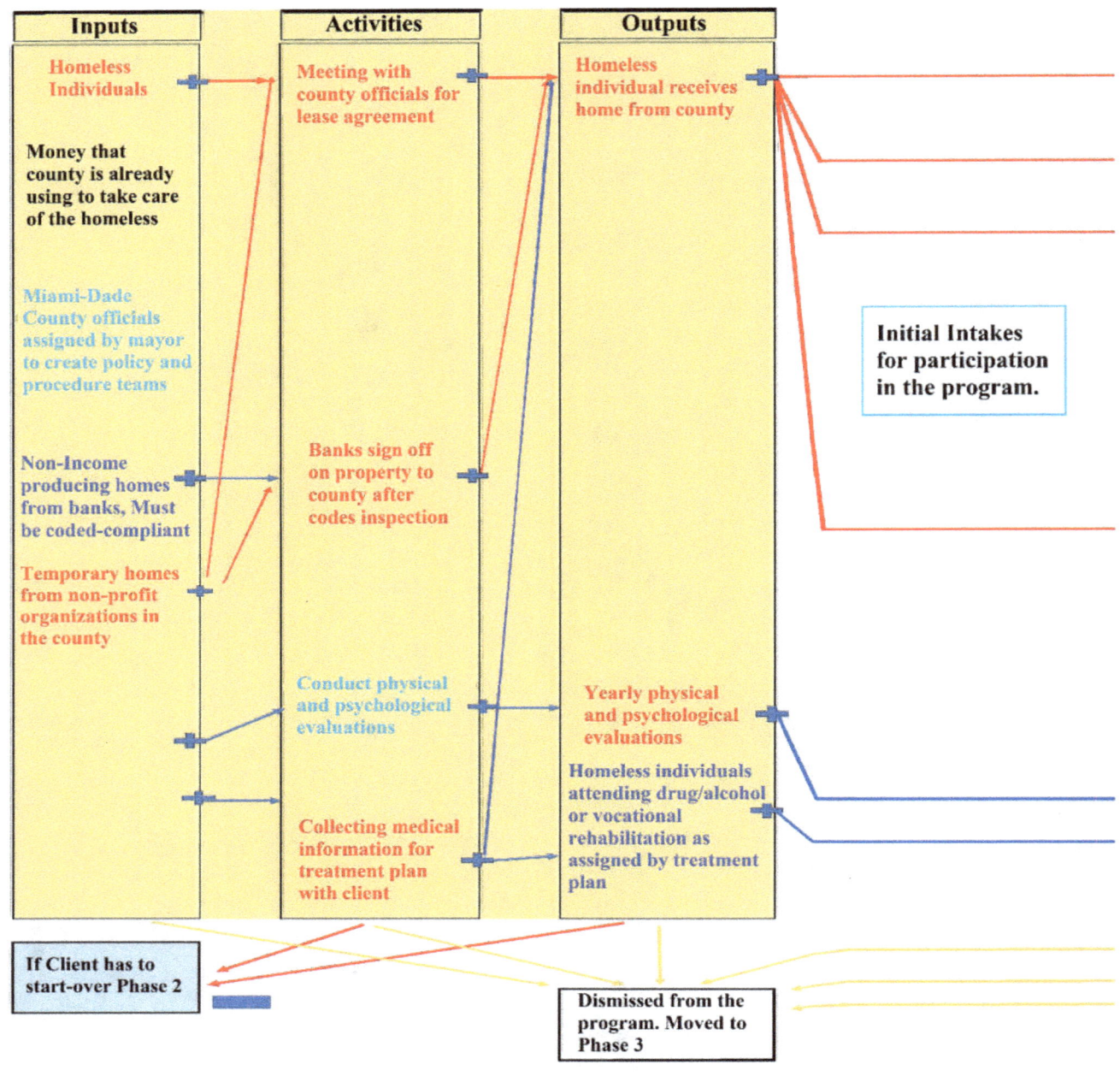

Chart 02 – Logic Model Stages

---

[23] Copyright Statement - From "Public Evaluation Design for Miami-Dade Home GAP," by J. Michael Montgomery and Sandro Alvarez, 2019: Unpublished manuscript. *Florida International University.* Adapted with permission.

1.08　Logic Model Stages 1. 2, 3, & 4 [24]

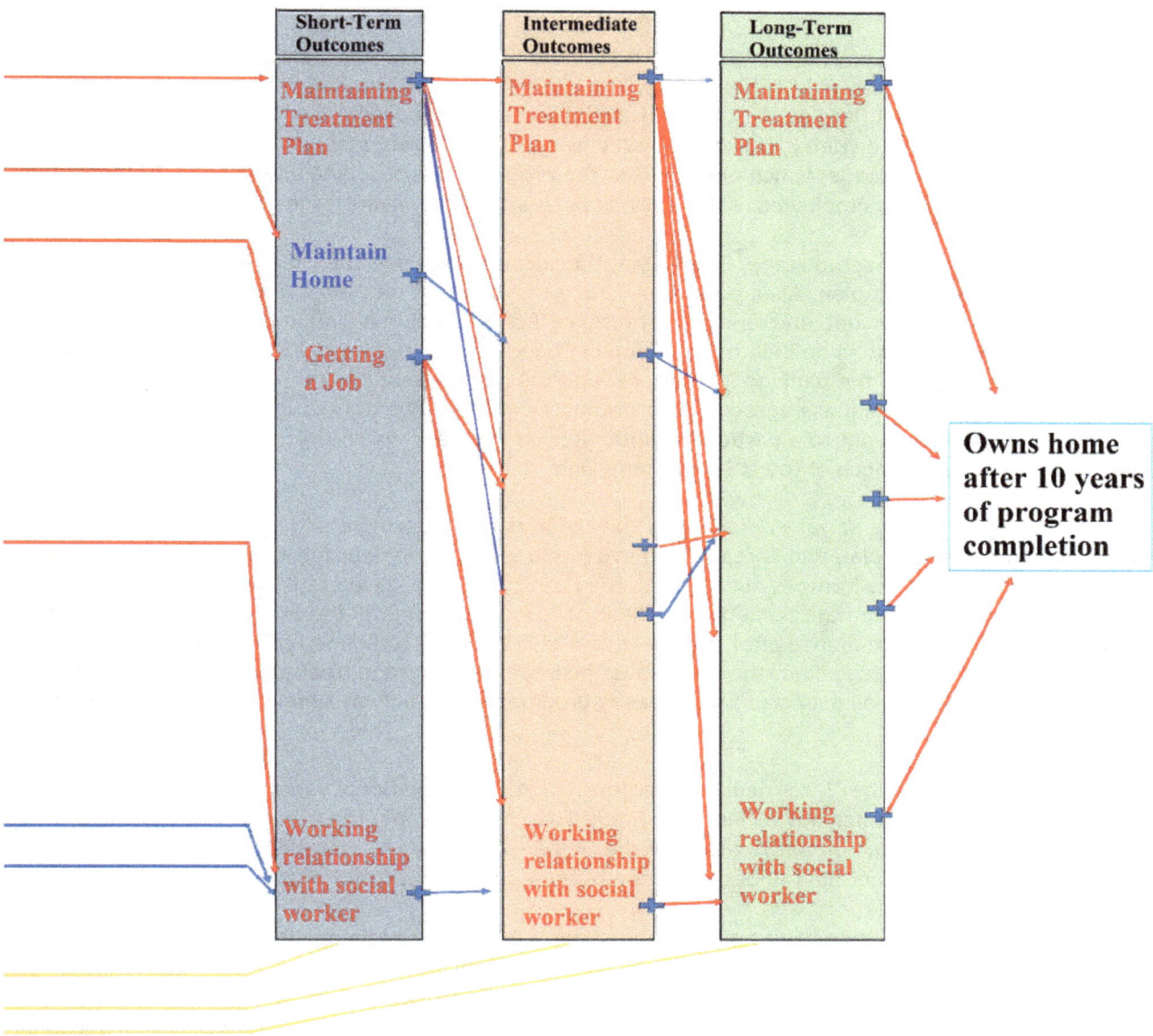

Chart 02 – Logic Model Stages

[24] Copyright Statement - From "Public Evaluation Design for Miami-Dade Home GAP," by J. Michael Montgomery and Sandro Alvarez, 2019: Unpublished manuscript. *Florida International University.* Adapted with permission.

1.09 Home GAP Initiative – Explaining the Logic Model

The program is a collaborative effort where multiple resources and personnel play essential roles in establishing the parameters of this program. The illustration as to how the program will be taken is in the form of a logic model. It is an illustration that showcases how a program will work and what the intended outcomes will be (Hatry, Newcomer, Wholey, 2015). [25] The model also contains positive indicators through each stage, which ensures that the program is functioning as intended. The negative integers come from non-compliance of the individuals in any of the given stages.

During the initial setup stage, Stage One, the social worker and the client are developing and working on the treatment plan. Also, during this stage, government officials will be developing a relationship with local banking and lending institution officials. To obtain livable homes from the bank's non-income producing list as defined by the Code of Federal Regulations §. 210.12–11, (ND).[26] Once homes are attained from the banking institutions, and the government has these homes, the government will prepare a lease agreement for the homes that will be utilized in the program. These homes will not be leased out to a participant until after two years when the client has completed the evaluation with the guidance of the MSW in Stage One.

In Stage Two, the social worker clears the client as having completed two years of participation in the agreed treatment plan and is ready to move into a lease agreement for a home in the Home GAP Program. At this time, the home is not gifted to the client; it will be leased to the client from the government agency. Gifting the home to the client does not happen until the end of Stage Four of the program and will only commence after the client has "successfully" completed all Home GAP requirements. While in Stage Two, the client must maintain their agreed treatment plan with their assigned MSW, maintain all aspects of their lease agreement, and actively obtain a job or maintain their disability treatment plan.

In Stage Three, the "Intermediate Outcome Stage," two additional years have passed for the client and social worker since advancing from Stage Two. At this stage, the client should be stable with the treatment plan entered into at the start of the Home GAP Initiative. The client must continue maintaining their treatment plan until completion of the entire Home GAP Initiative.

The client should now have a steady and stable job or is maintaining all requirements by their respective disability organization, such as Social Security Disability or, in the case of a veteran, the Veterans Administration Disability per VA regulations. Stage Three will last three years. The client should further his or her education, adding to their ability to get promotions in their career. This leading to an increase in their annual salary, thus, improving the community's GDP. Educational opportunities will be discussed between the client and the MSW. The client during Stage Three should demonstrate the ability to maintain their job.

---

[25] Newcomer, Kathryn E., Harry P. Hatry, and Joseph S. Wholey. Handbook of Practical Program Evaluation. 4th Ed. *Jossey-Bass; An Imprint of Wiley* (2015).
[26] Code of Federal Regulations. See Non-Income Producing Property. *Archives.Gov.* (n.d.).

Moreover, to preserve keeping and caring for their home. These participating individuals must continue to pay their obligated debts, including rent paid to the government agency per their lease agreement. Please note that as a participant in The Home GAP Initiative, clients will be classified as being in a "Homeless Status" until completion of this program. Also note that some states in the United States, as with the State of Florida has an educational law that helps all qualified homeless individuals with their educational needs.

In the 2019 Florida Statute Chapter 1009,[27] Educational Scholarships, Fees, and Financial Assistance (Online Sunshine, 2019), monetary payments are waived under (1)(f):

> "A student who lacks a fixed, regular, and adequate nighttime residence or whose primary nighttime residence is a public or private shelter designed to provide temporary residence, a public or private transitional living program, or a public or private place not designed for, or ordinarily used as, a regular sleeping accommodation for human beings. This includes a student who would otherwise meet the requirements of this paragraph, as determined by a college or university, but for his or her residence in college or university dormitory housing."

In Stage Four, the "Long-Term Outcome,"[28] an additional three years have passed, and in total, seven years have progressed in the "Home GAP Initiative" guidelines up to this point. The requirements and expectations that transpired during Stage Three will be the same during Stage Four. The client has demonstrated and met all the criteria set in The Home GAP Initiative. Upon completion of Stage Four, the client will be given the title and deed to the property that they have been living in since they signed their lease agreement — provided that the client maintains their treatment plan with the MSW and their lease agreement with the government.

After Stage Four, the client has demonstrated for the past ten years that they have established themselves as capable and productive tax-paying citizens for the community. Showing that they have contributed to their local community and have become a model citizen, and by adding their efforts to the GDP for the local government community, and have become an excellent tax-paying resident. It is at this moment that the government shall reward the client with the gift of the home. They are giving the client the title and deed to the property that they have been living in for the last eight years for their outstanding achievements since entering into The Home GAP Initiative.

If for some reason, the client fails at any stage of the Home GAP Initiative, the client will be reprocessed to start over at Stage Two of the Home Gap or will be transitioned out of the program and be evaluated for transitional housing. The MSW will determine the client's status and process them according to the rules set by the local government. All measurements in the reprocessed phase remain equivalent to the initial intaking. If the MSW deems that a client is to be dismissed from the program, then the client will then be sent to a temporary shelter and is then evaluated for transitional housing. A dismissal can happen at any stage of the program.

---

[27] Online Sunshine. The 2019 Florida Statues, Chapter 1009, Educational Scholarships, Fees, and Financial Assistance.
[28] Copyright Statement - From "Public Evaluation Design for Miami-Dade Home GAP," by J. Michael Montgomery and Sandro Alvarez, 2019: Unpublished manuscript. *Florida International University.* Adapted with permission.

1.10 Measures/Indicators – Phase I [29]

Chart 03 – Measures/Indicators – Phase I

Input	Activities	Output	Short-Term Outcome	Intermediate Outcome	Long-Term Outcome
Money that the county is already using to take care of homeless individuals. Measurement is taken in the amount of money that Miami-Dade County spends per year on homeless individuals. (Amount of $ spent per year). The goal is the reduction of money spent on every successful home placement. This is the Primary Indicator of a successful program.	Banks sign off the property to the county after the passage of codes inspection on the home. The measurement taken is the number of homes donated during the 10-years of this program. (# of homes donated). The goal is to provide more homes by bank donations, and the local government is to provide tax incentives to banks participating in this program.	Homeless individuals are receiving home from the county. Measurement is the number of lease agreements made and ready for occupation. (# of lease agreements).	Maintain the home given to the individual by the county. The indicator of maintenance of the leased property is by the number of visitations performed by the social worker (once a month required). Measured in the # of passed inspection on the document that both parties are being accountable.	We are enhancing personal and financial knowledge for homeless individuals. Indicator of success to be measured by how much money has the individual saved after three years from receiving the home. Although there are no criteria for how much money saved is deemed successful, any amount saved illustrates stability.	Maintain the home given to the individual by the county. The indicator of maintaining compliance is by the total number of visitations performed by the social worker (once a month required). Measured in the # that documents those individuals have passed the inspections by both parties to ensure that both parties are being accountable after an additional three more years from the intermediate to the end of the program.
Homeless individuals Measurement is the number of homeless individuals who have been located by the exceptional teams assigned by the Mayor for implementation of this program. (# of individuals recruited for the program by incentivizing them of benefits).	**We are collecting medical information for the client's treatment plan.** Measured by the number of approved treatment plans between social worker and client. (# of projects accepted in 1 year – should be equal to the total number enrolled).	Individuals are attending vocational or required medical workshops. The program aims to measure the number of clients who have agreed to treatment programs with social workers after two years (# of clients who agreed).	Individuals are attending vocational or required medical workshops. Across the board to measure if individuals are complying with their treatment plan after two years.	Individuals are attending vocational or required medical workshops. Across the board to measure individuals who are complying with their treatment plan after three years. The numbers should be equal.	Individuals are attending vocational or required medical workshops. Across the board to measure if individuals are complying with their treatment plan after an additional three more years. The numbers should remain equal. This point reaches ten years.

Measures/Indicators – Phase I, (Montgomery & Alvarez, 2019).

1.11   Measures/Indicators – Phase II [30]

Chart 04 – Measures/Indicators – Phase II

Input	Activities	Output	Short-Term Outcome	Intermediate Outcome	Long-Term Outcome
Money that the county is already using to take care of homeless individuals. Measurements taken are in the amount of money that Miami-Dade County spends per year on homeless individuals. (amount of $ spent per year) The goal is the reduction of money spent on every successful home placement — indicator of a successful program.	Banks sign off the property to the county after passing codes inspections on the home. Measurement is taken the number of homes donated in the span of 10 years. (# of homes donated). The goal is to provide more homes, and the local government is to provided tax incentives to participating banks.	Homeless individuals are receiving home from the county. The measurement is the number of lease agreements made and ready for occupation. (# of the records).	Maintain the home given to the individual by the county. The indicator of maintenance is by the number of visitations performed by the social worker (once a month required). Measured in # to document if both parties are being accountable.	We are enhancing personal and financial knowledge. Indicator of success to be measured by how much money has the individual saved after three years from receiving home. Although there are no criteria for how much money saved is deemed successful, any amount saved illustrates stability.	Maintain the home given to the individual by the county. The indicator of maintenance is by the number of visitations performed by the social worker (once a month required). Measured in # to document if both parties are being accountable after an additional three more years from the intermediate.
Homeless individuals Measurement in the number of homeless individuals enrolled by the exceptional team assigned by the Mayor has recruited. (# of individuals recruited for the program by incentivizing them of benefits).	We are collecting medical information for the individuals' treatment plan. They are measured by the number of approved treatment plans between the social worker and their assigned client. (# of plans approved in 1 year).	Individuals are attending vocational or required medical workshops. They are measured by the number of clients who have agreed to treatment programs with social workers after two years. (# of clients who agreed).	Individuals are attending vocational or required medical workshops. Across the board to measure if individuals are continually complying with their treatment plan after two years.	Individuals are attending vocational or required medical workshops. Across the board to measure if individuals are continually complying with their treatment plan after three years. The numbers should be equal.	Individuals are attending vocational or required medical workshops. Across the board to measure if individuals are continually complying with their treatment plan after an additional three more years. The numbers should remain equal.

Measures/Indicators – Phase II, (Montgomery & Alvarez, 2019).

1.12   Measures/Indicators – Phase III [31]

Chart 05 – Measures/Indicators – Phase III

Input	Activities	Outcome
Money that the county is already using to take care of homeless individuals. Measurement is taken in the amount of money that Miami-Dade County spends per year on homeless individuals. (Amount of $ spent per year) The goal is the reduction of money spent by the county for every successful home placement. Reduced Spending for the County is the Key Indicator for a successful program.	**Banks sign over the property to the county after passing codes inspection on the home.** Measurement is the number of homes donated in a span of 10 years. (# of homes donated). The goal is to provide more homes, and the local government is to provided tax incentives to participating banks. Phase 3 contains no output as homeless individuals do not receive a home when disenrolled from this program.	**Homeless individuals sent back to temporary shelters as the final permanent outcomes.** The measurement is the number of homeless individuals sent back to temporary shelters. (# of individuals sent to a temporary shelter).
Homeless individuals Measurement in the number of homeless individuals the special team assigned by the Mayor has recruited. (# of individuals recruited for the program by incentivizing them of benefits).	**We are collecting medical information for the treatment plan.** Measured by the number of approved treatment plans between social worker and client. (# of plans accepted in 1 year).	**The number of treatment plans revoked by the social worker.** Measure by the number of plans canceled to compare the data of those who completed the program). (# of plans removed by a social worker.

Measures/Indicators – Phase III, (Montgomery & Alvarez, 2019).

These are individuals who failed a re-evaluation or
who are non-compliant at any stage of the program.

1.13　Content Variables [32]

Possible influential factors:

1. The number of items that are in a treatment plan.
2. Not all treatment plans will be the same.
3. The region is an influential factor for space limitation and the assumption that homeless individuals will start coming to Miami-Dade County at a rapid pace, once the word gets out that Miami-Dade is giving homes to the homeless.
4. The number of non-income producing homes available for this program.

[32] Copyright Statement - From "Public Evaluation Design for Miami-Dade Home GAP," by J. Michael Montgomery and Sandro Alvarez, 2019: Unpublished manuscript. *Florida International University.* Adapted with permission.

1.14 Measures/Indicators – Client Intakes/Outputs [33]

Chart 06 – Measures/Indicators – Client Intakes/Outputs

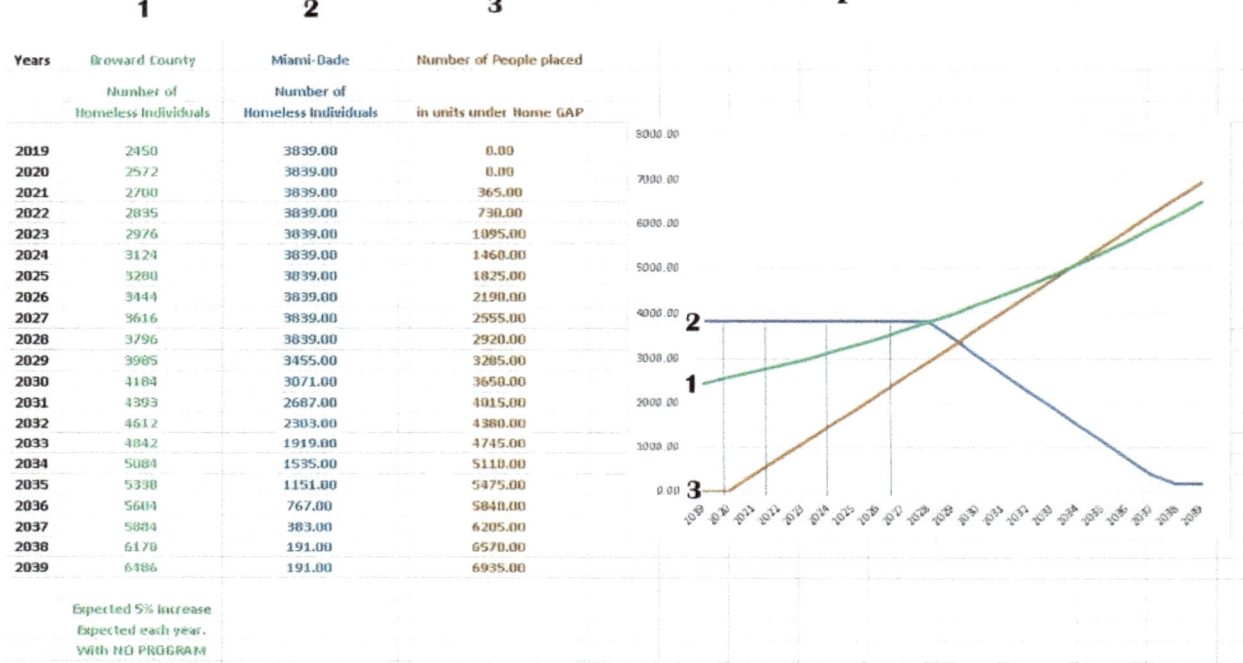

Client Intakes/Outputs

Years	1 Broward County Number of Homeless Individuals	2 Miami-Dade Number of Homeless Individuals	3 Number of People placed in units under Home GAP
2019	2450	3839.00	0.00
2020	2572	3839.00	0.00
2021	2700	3839.00	365.00
2022	2835	3839.00	730.00
2023	2976	3839.00	1095.00
2024	3124	3839.00	1460.00
2025	3280	3839.00	1825.00
2026	3444	3839.00	2190.00
2027	3616	3839.00	2555.00
2028	3796	3839.00	2920.00
2029	3985	3455.00	3285.00
2030	4184	3071.00	3650.00
2031	4393	2687.00	4015.00
2032	4612	2303.00	4380.00
2033	4842	1919.00	4745.00
2034	5084	1535.00	5110.00
2035	5338	1151.00	5475.00
2036	5604	767.00	5840.00
2037	5884	383.00	6205.00
2038	6178	191.00	6570.00
2039	6486	191.00	6935.00

Expected 5% Increase Expected each year. With NO PROGRAM INTERVENTION.

Measures/Indicators – Client Intakes/Outputs, (Montgomery & Alvarez, 2019).

1.15   Measures/Indicators – Government Expenditures [34]

Chart 07 – Measures/Indicators – Government Expenditures

Government Expenditures

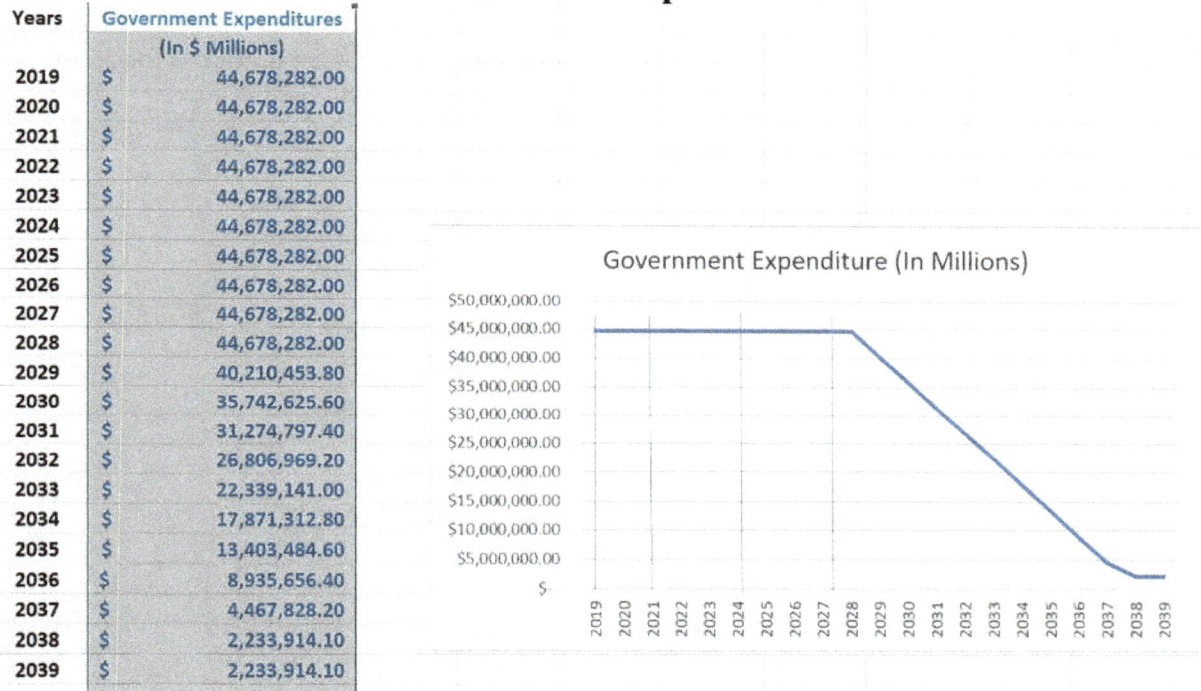

Years	Government Expenditures (In $ Millions)
2019	$ 44,678,282.00
2020	$ 44,678,282.00
2021	$ 44,678,282.00
2022	$ 44,678,282.00
2023	$ 44,678,282.00
2024	$ 44,678,282.00
2025	$ 44,678,282.00
2026	$ 44,678,282.00
2027	$ 44,678,282.00
2028	$ 44,678,282.00
2029	$ 40,210,453.80
2030	$ 35,742,625.60
2031	$ 31,274,797.40
2032	$ 26,806,969.20
2033	$ 22,339,141.00
2034	$ 17,871,312.80
2035	$ 13,403,484.60
2036	$ 8,935,656.40
2037	$ 4,467,828.20
2038	$ 2,233,914.10
2039	$ 2,233,914.10

Measures/Indicators – Government Expenditures (Montgomery & Alvarez, 2019).

[34] Copyright Statement - From "Public Evaluation Design for Miami-Dade Home GAP," by J. Michael Montgomery and Sandro Alvarez, 2019: Unpublished manuscript. *Florida International University.* Adapted with permission.

1.16 Ways to Mitigate Homelessness for the Government

There are several strategies adopted by the federal and local governments to try and control the situation where most of the efforts established have acted as a short-term solution in addressing the homelessness problem. With the assessment of the three available project evaluations (Montgomery, 2019)[35], it is clear that the third project with banks and financial institutions in donating homes to the homeless is preferable. It would help in maximizing the benefit-cost ratio for Miami-Dade. Therefore, since Program 3 has the highest NPV[36], The Home Giveaway Program Initiative (Home GAP) should be adopted in addressing the problem of homelessness for any state.

Program 3 is the best choice in combating homelessness, and it can be used as a model for other states to implement in reducing their numbers of homelessness within their borders.

---

[35] Copyright Statement - From "Reducing Homelessness in Miami-Dade County," by J. Michael Montgomery: Unpublished manuscript from Florida International University. Copyright 2019. Adapted with permission.
[36] R. S. Clemons. *"Public policy praxis: A case approach for understanding policy and analysis."* London Routledge. (2017).

Chapter 2

2.01   Theoretical Framework [37]

According to Montgomery (2019), long-term solutions, which are those that last for more than five years, are appropriate to eradicate homelessness in the United States and around the world. As Homeless Trust (2019) considers the "Point-in-Time" count, it credits an aggressive action to focus on long-term solutions that will ensure that homelessness can be addressed not only in Miami-Dade County but in other locations as well.

Although the homeless population could be considered relatively low, an analysis by the National Law Center on Homelessness and Poverty outlines that the actual community facing displacement might be between two to ten times higher than the point in time estimates. With a view on the adopted budget by the Homeless Trust as per the 2017-18 Fiscal year approved budget, there is sufficient funding to resolve the problem of homelessness in the County of Miami-Dade. However, the failure to spend all the money has been a trend in most of the previous budget cycles, where the trust did not spend approximately $23 million (Homeless Trust, 2019). Addressing the issues on budget spending, it is critical to consider this long-term solution aimed at maintaining affordable housing since it is likely to deliver a notable decline in homelessness.

Homelessness can be investigated through the concepts of social structure, social interaction, deviation, culture, and socialization as well. As the study is aimed at addressing the issue of homelessness and considering the long-term solution, then homelessness can be considered as social status (Tsai et al., 2017). Here, homelessness can be linked to poverty, stratification, and social exclusion and could also help understand the mobility of homelessness.

Although all theories of social conflict, structural functionalism, exchange, and symbolic interactionism can be applied in the study of homelessness, the theory of conflict and functionalism would be useful as they consider the paradigm of social fact (Shaw & Choi, 2019). With the focus of developing a long-term solution, any government agency ought to address the social conflict paradigm associated with the cost of housing—I.e., "Not In My Backyard" attitude towards homeless individuals.

Nonetheless, this theoretical 10-year program known as The Home Giveaway Program Initiative could be developed to assist in significantly reducing the numbers of those who are homeless (Montgomery, 2019). The Home GAP Initiative is designed to provide affordable housing for the unsheltered and homelessness in any government agency's jurisdiction. The Home Giveaway Program Initiative is a social project involving community members and various stakeholders that want to affect change for the homeless population. Within the Home GAP Initiative, the homeless individuals have to undergo a unique program to certify their suitability for owning a home, through their sobriety and develop a sense of responsibility through different tests with the guidance and structure set forth with an MSW. Also, through the participation of the 10-year educational program, a social worker will ensure that the individual acquires the necessary help to ensure that homelessness is addressed permanently.

---

[37] <u>Copyright Statement</u> - From "Long-Term Vs. Short-Term Solutions to Homelessness," by J. Michael Montgomery: Unpublished manuscript from Florida International University. Copyright 2020. Adapted with permission.

2.02 Research Question [38]

The issue of homelessness has delivered significant concerns as it remains an issue in Miami-Dade County and abroad. Often, this has been an issue due to the lack of proper assistive programs to help the unsheltered population. According to Semuels (2018), the different practices to reduce homelessness have been countered by various issues. They are equally resulting in other problems such as elevated poverty levels, insecurity, among other social and economic constraints. Where short-term solutions have been attempted, homelessness remains a significant issue in Miami-Dade County and throughout the rest of the United States. Thus, the research question will seek to evaluate the effectiveness of long-term solutions over short-term solutions to homelessness.

Research Question: Are long-term solutions to homelessness better than short-term solutions?

2.03 Methodology [39]

In the question of the effectiveness of long-term solutions over short-term solutions to eliminate homelessness, the factors influencing homelessness that play a significant role. In the case of Miami-Dade County, most of them are economically and socially associated, creating a need for a substantial initiative to address the problem completely. Short-term solutions are those that take less than five years, while long-term solutions such as The Home Giveaway Program Initiative take a minimum of 10 years (Montgomery, 2019). Even though the solution takes such a long time, this is continuous that not only looks at limiting the causes of homelessness but develop different initiatives that ensure that the homeless individuals are supported since they are vulnerable to other issues such as mental and health problems.

Through the use of short-term solutions to solve the problem of displacement, the primary focus is mounted on the reduction of the number of homeless individuals. Often, when the emphasis is placed on cutting down the numbers in the homeless populations, it is likely that some of the most critical elements could be ignored. Meanwhile, long-term solutions promote the empowerment of homeless individuals to solve a social conflict. Within the long-term solution, such as the Home GAP Initiative, it not only focuses on the needed medical and mental health treatment plans for a homeless individual but also is expanding affordable housing that is linked to other aspects.

Whereas short-term solutions do not break the cycle of homelessness as long-term solutions do, the long-term solution delivers significant developments as its initiatives integrate health care, strengthen the crisis response system, foster education, build career paths, and reduce criminal justice involvement. Through such a solution, these are likely to warrant a permanent solution to homelessness, then the homeless individuals in their respective communities can socially integrate with other aspects of the community.

2.04   Type of Research

This research will consider both quantitative and qualitative data associated with homelessness in Miami-Dade County and abroad. Within the quantitative analysis, it will involve collecting data through surveys and questionnaires to evaluate the number of homeless persons, government expenditures as it deals with eliminating homelessness, and the various benefits of the long-term Home GAP Initiative. Correspondingly, qualitative research will identify abstract concepts by comparing similar initiatives for use in other nations such as the:
Journey to Social Inclusion in Australia (J2SI).

2.05   Respondent Questionnaire (See Appendix B and C)

2.06   How Does Homelessness affect any community?

- What solutions are available for homelessness?
- What are the main reasons for homelessness?
- Can social policies be implemented to avoid such cases?

2.07 Hypothesis[40]

Long-term solutions to homelessness, such as The Home Giveaway Program Initiative, provides a holistic approach that is better than the short-term solutions. In the delivery of such a program, it is possible to integrate it with other plans such as the Homelessness Prevention and Rapid Re-Housing Program (HPRP). Also, The Home GAP Initiative allows integration with the Low-Income Housing Tax Credit (LIHTC), which deals with the developers of housing initiatives. In the long run, the long-term solution, The Home GAP Initiative, has to be economically feasible to offer significant results. Cunningham and Batko (2018), argued that the LIHTC should ensure that the initiative follows specified guidelines. It includes consultation with the local government agency's laws and policies. In the cost-benefit analysis of the program, the LIHTC could be integrated with The Home GAP Initiative to ensure that the developed shelters for the homeless individuals are below 30% of the AMI as per the United States Department of Housing and Urban Development (US Department of HUD, 2013).

Moreover, since the pattern of rural to urban migration in Miami-Dade County has accelerated the homelessness problem in Florida, particularly the Miami-Dade community, the banks, and other monetary lending organizations, together with legislators, need to help develop long-term initiatives (Turner 2019). Through financing, this can promote affordable housing since people can access loans to improve existing homes. Also, people can be given capital in the form of labor to aid them at affordable rates in case they have funds for building houses. According to Richardson (2019), it is significant for the banks to maintain a reasonably low-interest rate on loans since high-interest rates could worsen the situation. Mackenzie et al. (2017), added that efficiency in the real estate industry would significantly enhance affordable housing, which is the ultimate goal for Home GAP Initiative in the elimination of homelessness. Also, this explains the significance of long-term solutions to homelessness over short-term solutions.

In other ways, immigration may affect the research question concerning the effectiveness in the application of long-term solutions to eradicate homelessness compared to short-term solutions. Often, immigrants arriving in America are likely to face continuous discrimination as they are forced into low skilled and low paying jobs, which creates instability and a socio-economic disadvantage. Such activities could result in homelessness as most immigrants could be displaced. For example, according to the Center on Human Rights Education, the homeless population rose to 46,874 people in Los Angeles, a 6% increase, where a large portion of the homeless individuals are immigrants (Galley, 2018).

However, this brings about the application for the use of The Home GAP Initiative in Miami, other cities in the US, and other countries can adapt the program to address homelessness among its populations and immigrants as well.

Chapter 3

3.01   The Problem of Homelessness in the US

The problem of homelessness has become more significant in today's society and raises those alarms where various stakeholders are concerned. Gregerson (2013) stated that:

> *"the attempts of reducing the homeless population are always faced with significant challenges since the causes are complex and difficult to understand."*

The homeless population is diverse; they consist of men, women, and families with children, unlike in the past when the majority of the homeless inhabitants were comprised of mostly adult males. The problem is accelerated current shortages of affordable housing and elevated levels of poverty, which makes it difficult for low- or no-income people not meeting their living expenses. Others are also living with no home due to their physical and mental conditions.[41]

3.02   Domestic Violence and Homelessness [42]

Domestic violence is a global issue that is at the core of most states' boundaries, racial, cultural, socio-economic issues, and class distinctions. These broad and deeply embedded issues affect men's and women's well-being and health. Domestic violence has long-been ignored and not well understood by many (Johnson, Ribar, and Zhu, 2017).[43] However, with the issue of chronic homelessness increasing, domestic violence is one of the leading reasons associated with homelessness among men, women, and children. Any person affected by concerns of domestic violence is to leave their homes.

They may suffer the psychological and physical consequences; the cost of staying at home is too painful to continue to endure (Wright, 2017). Most societal systems view homelessness negatively and determine the impact that this issue has on various regions that affect the growth of the area.

---

[41] A. Gregerson. *"Homelessness presents numerous problems for South Florida."* News Reporting & the Internet. (2013).

[42]

[43] Johnson, Ribar, and Zhu. "Women's Homelessness: International Evidence on Causes, Consequences, and Policies." IZA. Institute of Labor Economics. (2017).

3.03   Drug and Alcohol Abuse and Homelessness [44]

The correlation between homelessness and addiction may seem controversial as viewed by California (specifically San Francisco) with their issues; that some Californians are experiencing have been brought to light by the media (Chakraborty, 2019) though there is an exceedingly high rate of drugs and alcohol abuse among homeless people. Individuals who are drug addicts may not become homeless, but in most cases, persons who are sick and addicted have a high likelihood of becoming homeless.

Homeless individuals have faced stressful situations such as financial setbacks, family conflicts, and lack of proper housing and care for children involved. Facing the realization that one may become homeless, results in mental health struggles and further addictions concerns that impede the ability of the family unit to attain a stable life.

3.04   Alcoholism, Drug Abuse, and Veterans with PTSD

Alcoholism, drug abuse, mental health issues, and in the case of veterans experiencing Post-Traumatic Stress Disorder (PTSD) (Cundiff, 2015),[45] has also been in the frontline for increasing the number of individuals living in a homelessness situation. Gregerson (2013) stated that in the year 2006, Miami-Dade had 4,709 people living without homes, while in 2007, the number reduced to 4,392.

While there was a rise in the total amount of homeless individuals in 2008, the actual number was not higher than that of the year 2007. By 2010 the number of homeless persons was 3,832 (Gregerson, 2013), which is represented in the next chart.

Veterans who are accepted into the Home GAP Initiative will be admitted regardless of their level of medical, mental health, or discharge status: This is the same as how the Kansas City, Missouri program is operating (Village of Tiny Homes Built for Homeless Veterans In Kansas City, 2018).[46]

---

[44] Copyright Statement -   From "Reducing Homelessness in Miami-Dade County," by J. Michael Montgomery: Unpublished manuscript from Florida International University. Copyright 2019. Adapted with permission.
[45] S, Cundiff. *"Veterans and Addictions: Homelessness and Post-Traumatic Stress Disorder."* Commonwealth of Ky. (2015).
[46] Village of Tiny Homes Built for Homeless Veterans In Kansas City. (2018).

3.05　Miami-Dade Statistics for Homeless Population

Chart 08 - Homeless Bar Graph

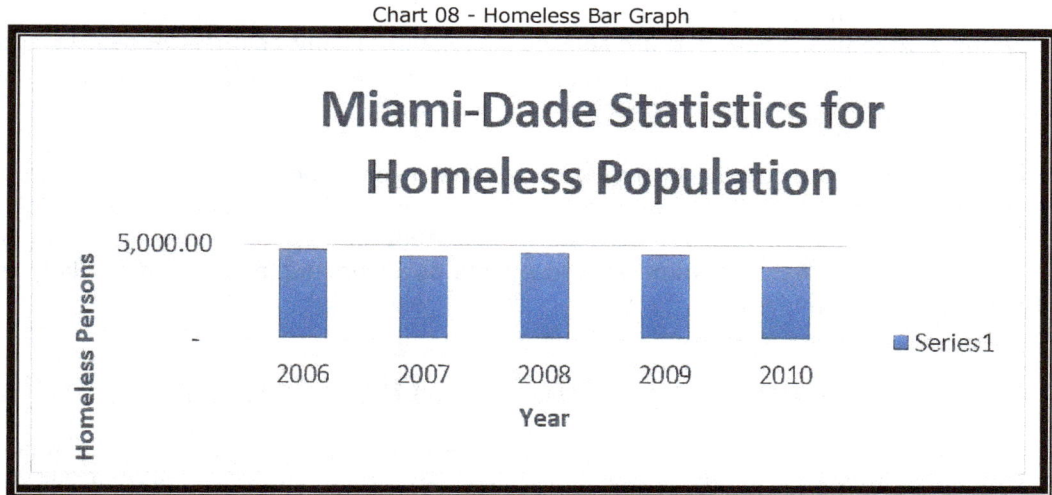

Homeless Bar Graph (Gregerson, 2013). [47]

---

[47] A. Gregerson. "*Homelessness presents numerous problems for South Florida.*" News Reporting & the Internet. 2013).

3.06   Inefficient Social Protection Systems [48]

The capability of an individual, especially to build and maintain a self-governing household, has been proven to be dependent on the status of their family's situation. They face the degree to which they can access protection to keep their home and face one's financial struggles. Social welfare plays a significant part in the configuration of the displaced population in any country. Access to appropriate, affordable healthcare facilities represents a high priority role in how the head of the household takes care of their families.

Also, a society that provides social support, including income security, employment opportunities, and protection from loss of primary income, can guarantee reducing homelessness and possibly the non-occurrence of homelessness (Utržan, Piehler, Gewirtz, & August, 2017). The lack of such a system, families, and individuals will become vulnerable in events of adversities and will most likely result in a high priority of becoming homeless.

3.07   Social Displacement through Disasters and Conflicts [49]

Dislocation is a result of natural disasters and clashes. Although, situations through which an individual is rendered homeless or displaced experience the same conditions. Both displacements by conflict and by a natural disaster can result in the loss of family members, separation from family members, loss of their possessions, will in most cases, experience depression and trauma. Families are further subjected to the biases in the provision of assistance, discrimination in the provision of aid, and most likely forced relocation.

A natural disaster, as with the catastrophic event associated with Hurricane Katrina in 2005[50], displaced over 800,000 individuals into a homelessness status. Two hundred thousand homes were destroyed, of those homes destroyed 41,000 were designated as rental units. As of 2005, eighty thousand dwellings remained vacant for various reasons. Two hundred thirty thousand jobs were lost in the job market for Louisiana (Admin, 2009). As earlier described, there are many different definitions of the term homeless. Most individuals affected by displacements from their dwellings in the aftermath of Hurricane Katrina prefer to be known as "Homeless Homeowners."

3.08   Mental Health and Homelessness [51]

Approximately 22% of lone adults are homeless, suffer from severe and unrelenting mental illness.[52] Homelessness strengthens the issues of those who are dealing with mental illness. The experience of stress and trauma linked to homelessness can result in depression, fear, possible substance abuse, or even thoughts of suicide. Even death does occur because the homeless individual has given up all hope. Despite that, the rise in the number of homeless individuals dealing with mental issues not released from health institutions compounds a patient's anxiety associated with homelessness. Most of the ill-health individuals who are also homeless are, in most cases, unable to access either supportive housing or medical treatment (Zufferey, 2016). The provision of affordable and adequate shelter allocated to homeless people will help in minimizing, coping with, and reducing incidents of mental illness. Also, the government should provide them with adequate food supply and medical care services.

3.09   Miami Homelessness Census Reveals

The homeless census reveals that there are 3,839 homeless people in Miami-Dade (Ullman, 2016).[53] This news release shows that a total of 3,526 residents were homeless in Miami-Dade as of the year 2018. They are costing Miami-Dade $12,671 per person as it takes care of each of those homeless individuals, totaling $44,678,282 each year. Miami experienced an 8% decrease from the previous year, where about 321 individuals found solutions to their homelessness (Mozloom, 2018).[54] Also, the report by Mozloom reveals that 75% of the unsheltered persons are men, 44% of the unsheltered individuals are those with no source of income, and 38% of those are vulnerable persons who are individuals with disabilities.

The decline in the number of homeless indicates the effectiveness of the efforts put in place to solve the problem of homelessness. The decrease in this rate is much slighter and hence, is still leaving a significant population with no safe and affordable shelter. Given the above statistics, the magnitude of the problem is still considerable, showing that the agencies concerned ought to respond appropriately in understanding and mitigating all of the issues where homelessness occurs.

---

[51] Copyright Statement -   From "Reducing Homelessness in Miami-Dade County," by J. Michael Montgomery: Unpublished manuscript from Florida International University. Copyright 2019. Adapted with permission.
[52] D. Padgett. "Housing First: Ending Homelessness, Transforming Systems and Changing Lives." Focus Consulting, Inc. (2013).
[53] Ullman. "STATE OF FLORIDA REPORT: 2016 Homeless Census Estimates and Funding Need to End Chronic Homelessness.
[54] L. Mozloom. "Miami-Dade County - Homeless Trust." News Release. (2018).

3.10   Adequate Housing Policies

The United Nations[55] identifies homelessness as a developing issue worldwide. It is a human right to have a formal shelter. According to Leilani Farha (Phillips, 2015), the proper acceptable housing must be viewed just like the right to live in peace at a given place. With dignity and adequate security, such as an efficient housing program, should encompass the protection of ownership, service availability, affordability, accessibility, cultural, and location adequacy. With the achievement of sufficient housing, then homelessness will not be occurring. The United Nations members devoted themselves to ending homelessness and gradually being acquainted with the rights to ample shelter through their obligation to the New Urban Agenda (2017).[56]

Tackling the homeless issue is essential in achieving the vision of the "Habitat Agenda" in both the public and private sectors (Toepfer, 2000). The progress in attaining the desired result for the elimination of homelessness sometimes may interfere with the success and attainment of different goals. Families who are affected by homelessness, are mostly categorized among the susceptible population whose conditions are worsened by their incapacity to access public services. With no proper way to address their challenges, often, these people, including their families, struggle to get essential services, even including the most basic items to satisfy their needs. Research shows that poverty is a common denominator in the familiarities of homelessness.

Sound social policies have contributed significantly to the reduction in homeless families worldwide (Mago, Vijay, et al., 2013). It has demonstrated that gender and family sensitive social safety policies and initiation of programs that are causally linked with the effectiveness of the designed systems to reduce family homelessness.

---

[55] K. Toepfer. "Strategies to Combat Homelessness." United Nations Human Settlements (Habitat). Nairobi. (2000).
[56] Habitat3.org. (2017). "New Urban Agenda." Authorized by Dr. Joan Clos. Secretary-General of the United Nations Conference on Housing and Sustainable Urban Development (Habitat III).

Internationally, there has been the establishment of public and national support programs, which has been the most successful housing solution in the reduction of homeless individuals. It has enabled housing to be affordable to vulnerable individuals. This housing program has been a success in reducing the number of homeless individuals. For instance, in the Netherlands[57], they presented direct monetary assistance to most of the qualified renters (I Am Expat, n.d.). This initiative gave the government a blueprint for which to tackle their societal issue on homelessness.

The compassionate housing model put together the housing support and assistance for persons and families who are living with mental illness (Johnson, Ribar, & Zhu, 2017).[58] The majority of the countries' housing initiatives are carried out by the civil sector, private investments, and the public sector. These contributors have played a role in the current level of resources needed to sustain emergencies of health, institutional services, and accommodations. It is not enough to deal with rising levels of living at the poverty level. Families who are vulnerable and are homeless are among the susceptible population. For this reason, the housing model addresses their challenges to combat their struggle to getting their essential services to satisfy a homeless person's needs.

---

[57] I Am Expat. "Rental Security Deposits In The Netherlands." IAMEXPAT. (n.d.)
[58] Johnson, Ribar, & Zhu. "Women's Homelessness: International Evidence on Causes, Consequences, and Policies." IZA. Institute of Labor Economics. (2017).

Chapter 4

4.01   HPRP, Home GAP, and LIHTC [59]

The integration of (HPRP) Homelessness Prevention and Rapid Re-Housing Program (Carson, 2019)[60] , in conjunction with The Home Giveaway Program Initiative (Home GAP)[61], if implemented by the Miami-Dade government, will be crucial in reducing the issue of homelessness. Integration of all state and federal regulations will be vital in offering this ten-year long-term solution to the problem of homelessness as current laws will fully back The Home GAP Initiative.

The Low-Income Housing Tax Credit (LIHTC)[62] will play a significant role in providing developers' reasonable terms. This, in turn, will be crucial in developing the Home GAP Initiative to the needs for placement of those individuals in the Home GAP as set forth by the Miami-Dade government to comply with standards and codes to guide the program to fruition. According to Cunningham & Batko (2018), [63] LIHTC will enable developers in the market who happen to obtain the tax credit award would have a limited stake of ownership of the properties. Thereby implementing and utilizing The Home GAP Initiative following developed guidelines by Miami-Dade County government officials will be beneficial to all stakeholders.

However, the investors from the LIHTC will be subjected to having an eight to ten-year limited stake of ownership of homes in The Home GAP Initiative that are being established in Miami-Dade. In this case, the local government (Miami-Dade) will have a hand in dictating housing terms for these participants. The state government will be crucial in ensuring that the housing rates in the market do not place a burden on the participants in The Home GAP Initiative.

4.02   The Government is the frontline

The state and local governments have been on the frontline in offering arguments on homeless initiative programs. The LIHTC will be crucial in addressing the high number of homeless people in Miami-Dade. The Home GAP Initiative project has argued that it will be critical to ensuring that homeless people in Miami-Dade can be taken care of on a humanitarian level.

---

[59] US Department of HUD. "Programs of HUD," (2016).
[60] B. Carson. *Homelessness Prevention Rapid Re-Housing Program. HUD. (2019).*
[61] Copyright Statement - From "Reducing Homelessness in Miami-Dade County," by J. Michael Montgomery: Unpublished manuscript from Florida International University. Copyright 2019. Adapted with permission.
[62] A. Schwartz. *"Housing policy in the United States (3rd edition)."* NY, NY: Routledge. (2015).
[63] M, Cunningham. S, Batko. *"Rapid Re-housing's Role in Responding to Homelessness."* Metropolitan Housing and Communities Policy Center. (2018).

4.03   Acquiring Shelter for Homeless Individuals

Homeless individuals will be able to acquire shelter. Addressing the issue of homelessness, and having those enrolled participants play an active role in The Home GAP Initiative; thus, being reintegrated back into society as proud and fruitful citizens. Homeless persons who choose to participate in The Home GAP Initiative that has low- or no-income will be required to participate in specialized health and work-related programs.

The criteria for this participation will be set up by Miami-Dade officials.[64] The intended goal of The Home Giveaway Program Initiative (Home GAP) is to have a well-constructed plan, that, after ten years, will allow an individual to go from being homeless to becoming a long-term, productive, tax-paying citizen, and eventually, a mortgage-paying homeowner.

The Low-Income Housing Tax Credit[65] will play a significant role in creating rent restrictions in the housing market of Miami-Dade. In most current housing markets, the housing rents and rates are usually determined by the various forces that are integrated into the housing market. The rent restrictions will be crucial in creating rent ceilings, which will uphold a maximum amount of rent that is payable by The Home GAP Initiative applicants in the Miami-Dade market.

The LIHTC will play a significant role in guaranteeing that any home unit falling under LIHTC and through The Home GAP Initiative, does not exceed 30% of the Area Median Income (AMI),[66] which happens to be adjusted per the size of the family. The Home GAP Initiative strategy will be essential in ensuring that the various housing unit's rental prices in the market are not over-priced (Winch, 2011). This plan will be crucial in reducing homelessness in Miami-Dade, as most individuals in The Home GAP Initiative will have the ability to afford the housing rates in the market (Cunningham & Batko, 2018). This will ensure that the costs that are incurred in the development of gifted homes for The Home GAP Initiative need to be considerably and comparatively lower for the benefits accrued from this project.

---

[64] Copyright Statement -   From "Reducing Homelessness in Miami-Dade County," by J. Michael Montgomery: Unpublished manuscript from Florida International University. Copyright 2019. Adapted with permission.
[65] A. Schwartz. *"Housing policy in the United States."* (3rd edition). New York, NY: Routledge. (2015).
[66] U.S. Department of Housing and Urban Development Office of Policy Development and Research. *"Strategies for improving homeless people's access to mainstream benefits and services."* US Department of HUD. (2013).

4.04 Strategies for an Effective Initiative of The Home GAP

Strategies need to be created, which will be essential in ensuring that the various needs of the homeless populace are addressed in The Home GAP community. This project will be crucial in developing these homes through the first two years and then through the rest of the stages of The Home GAP Initiative. With the rest of the project to expand within ten years, this will lead to a reduction of homelessness among individuals in Miami-Dade (Lopez & Froese, 2016).[67] Reducing homelessness with The Home Giveaway Program Initiative in Miami-Dade will be achieved through effective coordination among various officials and stakeholders. This will be critical in developing costs and benefits within a particular time.

The rising number of homeless individuals is a result of the inflated cost of housing that is witnessed in the Miami-Dade area and across the country. **LIHTC,** the Low-Income Housing Tax Credit (Schwartz, 2015),[68] is an indirect subsidy used by contractors to obtain finances to build or rehabilitate housing facilities. They are enabling the majority of the low- or no-income individuals living in Miami-Dade to get adequate housing through the county's Home Giveaway Program Initiative. Participating banks and financial institutions will donate these housing units (dubbed "Micro-Projects") to the county for distribution to the homeless that qualify.

The Home Giveaway Program Initiative would also be the best alternative to rehabilitate a considerable number of homes dubbed "Micro-Projects" with the LIHTC program. Emphasis will be placed on the donated homes in The Home GAP Initiative and will be managed by the Miami-Dade government, which in turn will be contracted out to local contractors to maintain compliance with The Home GAP Initiative, LIHTC rules, local, state, federal rules, and regulations. Most people belonging to the middle income and particularly the low-income social class usually find it challenging to afford the high rates and rents being demanded by property owners or housing agencies in the Miami-Dade area (VHA Office of Mental Health, 2012).[69]

The LIHTC will be crucial in ensuring that the housing sector integrates the needs of this category of individuals (Dietz, 2015)[70] by providing houses that are donated in The Home GAP Initiative that match the needs of those who are low- or no-income earners within the local economy.

---

[67] D. Lopez. *"Analysis of costs and benefits of panelized and modular prefabricated homes."* Science Direct. (2016).

[68] A. Schwartz. *"Housing policy in the United States."* NY, NY: Routledge. (2015).

[69] VHA Office of Mental Health. "Homeless Veterans." (2012).

[70] R. Dietz. *"How Many People Have Benefitted from the Affordable Housing Credit?"* NAHB. (2015).

Chapter 5

5.01   Reducing Economic Issues through Problem-Solving

Research conducted by Atuheire & Karyeija (2014)[71] revealed that the problem of homelessness is far more severe with low-income earners. The study conducted in Kampala Uganda confirmed that the most significant cause of homelessness is affordability. The same case applies to Miami-Dade, whereas the numbers of homeless people are high due to inadequate housing options. This homeless group highly relies on grants and donations for their survival. Thus, calling for many volunteers who are aiding the less fortunate population in Miami-Dade in the attempt to address the immediate issues of homelessness.

Montgomery's (2019) research paper recommended Project 3[72] for the utilization of local banks and financial institutions to donate properties with which to reduce homelessness as the most viable alternative for solving this ongoing problem. The approach is associated with tremendous benefits, not only to the beneficiaries but also to all parties involved.

Banks may also tackle the issue by providing low-interest rate loans, which must be accessible to all of those in need of a home (Atuheire & Karyeija, 2014). These loans should not be determined based on the availability of the borrowers' collateral. Many individuals living below the poverty line do not possess significant assets. Therefore, asking those homeless individuals to provide security for their housing loans might discriminate them from accessing these vital facilities.

---

[71] K. Atuheire. *"The role of financial institutions towards affordable housing to urban middle-income earners."* (2014).
[72] <u>Copyright Statement</u> - From "Reducing Homelessness in Miami-Dade County," by J. Michael Montgomery: Unpublished manuscript from Florida International University. Copyright 2019. Adapted with permission.

5.02   Housing Cost Alternatives

In Florida, a significant amount of people are moving to more rural areas; this is defined as urban migration (Wiggins, 2007)[73]. People are flocking to developed cities in search of employment opportunities, which has created a shortage in the housing market. Establishing programs funded by the banks to construct, rehabilitate, or giveaway more homes will help in meeting the demand and hence reduce homelessness. Rural to urban migration has accelerated the problem of chronic homelessness in Miami-Dade. Hence, government officials should be looking at establishing a system of equitable distribution of resources that would also help in mitigating the problem. The recommendation for using The Home Giveaway Program Initiative is useful in this situation.

One approach whereby the banking sector can help in providing a solution to the problem is the insufficient access to affordable housing is by giving smaller loans for improving on existing homes. An additional course of action is to have banks avoid charging high-interest rates on the loans that are for funding associated with a home that worsens the living standards of low-income people (Richardson, 2019).[74]

---

[73] S, Wiggins. *"Rural employment and migration: In search of decent work."* Overseas Development Institute. (2007).
[74] B. Richardson. *"America's housing affordability crisis is only getting worse."* Forbes. (2019).

Those individuals having a large portion of their income associated with their homes are usually left with inadequate funds to care for such basic needs as food, clothes, water, and medical needs (Homelessness 101, 2019)[75].

Chart 09 – What Triggers Homelessness?

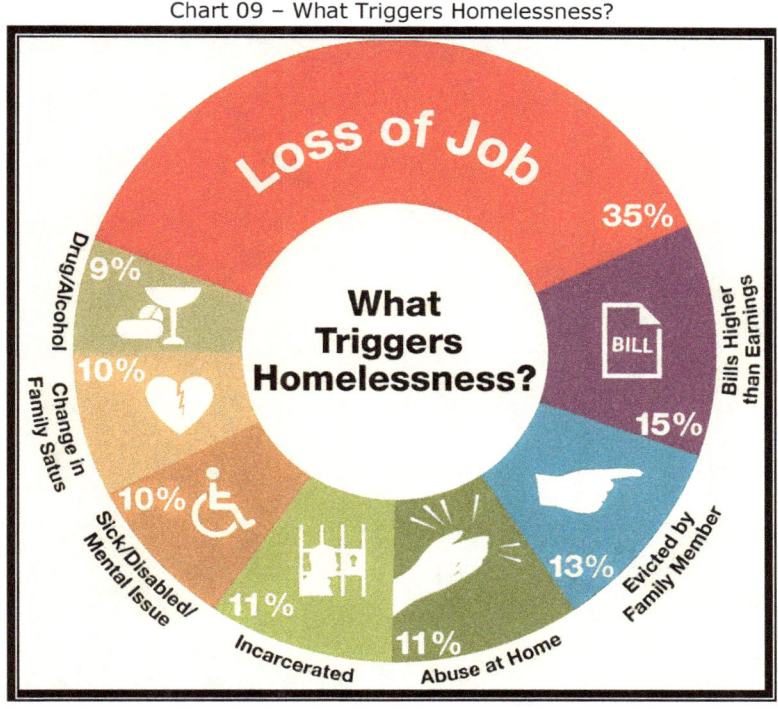

Homeless Bar Graph (Homelessness 101, 2019).

Mitlin (2007) argued that providing adequate capital to the real estate investors will help in expanding low-income shelters to accommodate the current market. [76] Richardson (2019) stated that:

> "housing affordability in 2012 was 78% based on the incomes and current interest rates. However, by the third quarter of 2018, that score of 78 had plummeted to 56, meaning only 56% of home sales were affordable."

Improving efficiency in the real estate sector will also help in reducing the housing prices and henceforth will make them affordable to the lower-income earners (MacKenzie, McNelis, Flatau, Valentine, & Seivwright. 2017).[77] The interest charged on borrowing is an allowable tax expense, which creates an incentive for the investors. It also lowers the perceived cost of capital and reduces the price charged to the tenants.

---

[75] Homelessness 101. "The face of homelessness has changed." Coalition for the Homeless. (2019).

[76] D. Mitlin. *Finance for low-income housing community development.* (2007).

[77] D. MacKenzie, S. McNelis, P. Flatau, K. Valentine, & A. Seivwright. *"The funding and delivery of programs to reduce homelessness: the case study evidence."* (2017).

Chapter 6

6.01 Banks Providing Humanitarian Actions

The banking sectors provide the best approach to addressing the persistent problem of homelessness. Humanitarian actions will involve local banks to be allowed to donate homes out of their non-income producing list to The Home Giveaway Program Initiative, which will, in turn, be managed by designated government officials. The project must have a mutual benefit to all the stakeholders involved. For example, the primary beneficiaries are low-income people living in Miami-Dade without homes. Additionally, the banks will benefit from the reduced tax liability since the project provides an excellent opportunity for corporate tax planning approaches. By concentrating on The Home GAP Initiative, the local government will experience decreasing expenditures in the allocations of taking care of the homeless community, while tax revenues are increasing.[78]

6.02 Banks Enhancing Their Corporate Image

Participating banks will be capable of enhancing their corporate image since the act of housing the homeless would be seen as a corporate social responsibility. They are being vital in creating that competitive advantage for the banking and lending institutions in an open market. Banks play a significant role in housing and financial institution initiatives through various approaches, such as the provision for cheaper mortgage loans, home donations, and direct investments in real estate, among other plans. It provides financial resources for real estate development. The act of banks donating homes through The Home GAP Initiative to the homeless makes it the most effective way of reducing homelessness in Miami-Dade and abroad.

6.03 Banking Institutions Venturing in Real Estate

The banking sector has been venturing into the real estate business where the living standards are improved for their members by providing access to affordable housing facilities. By putting the resources together, the banks are in a position of buying land and building housing units or rehabilitating or bringing up the homes designated to The Home GAP to local codes under LIHTC[79] at lower costs due to the benefit of the economies of the domestic arena. It helps in reducing the housing shortage existing due to the high demand for homes and the small number available that are considered as affordable homes.

---

[78] Copyright Statement - From "Reducing Homelessness in Miami-Dade County," by J. Michael Montgomery: Unpublished manuscript from Florida International University. Copyright 2019. Adapted with permission.
[79] A. Schwartz. "Housing Policy in the United States.". NY, NY: Routledge. (2015).

The banking sector should aim at establishing more affordable housing programs in the efforts of addressing the problem of the homeless, which has become much common in today's life. More specifically, the government should also play its role effectively to encourage banks to invest in the real estate market that targets low-income earners. The part that the government will play in this venture by promoting The Home Gap Initiative will benefit from the increased tax revenues generated.

6.04   Banking Trends

The study conducted by D'erasmo (2019)[80] on banking trends, concluded that the banks ought to adopt proper measures for them to survive the fluctuations in the commercial real estate market prices. The researcher argues that the real estate marketplace might impose a significant risk to the banks due to the high default rate. Banks that are showing that they are increasing their lending and gifting home programs in the viable real estate application process would spur that continuous growth for the community. Hence, using non-income producing properties for The Home GAP Initiative is the best solution to battling homelessness.

Commercial real estate capitalization increases significantly from one budget year to the other. However, the expected returns in the real estate market are falling, which discourages many investors from investing in this field. The resulting impact is the increase in the shortage of the existing real estate market, whereby the demand exceeds the supply (D'erasmo, 2019). By applying these economic theories, the immediate effect of this trend will increase the general price level of the home, making it impossible for the low-income earners to afford a place to live and thrive, and therefore ending up homeless. Effective measures must be adapted to lower and prevent housing prices from going up for local economies to ensure the attainment of a reduction in the homelessness problem (MacKenzie, McNelis, Flatau, Valentine, & Seivwright. 2017).[81]

The chart below shows the rent trends in Miami that are the average rent prices over the last three years. From this chart, it is clear that rent prices have gone up. This trend is expected to continue and hence reducing the affordability of homes for low-income individuals seeking a reasonably priced place to live.

[80] P. D'erasmo. "*Estimating Today's Commercial Real Estate Risk.*" Banking Trends. (2019).
[81] D. MacKenzie, S. McNelis, P. Flatau, K. Valentine, & A. Seivwright. "*The funding and delivery of programs to reduce homelessness: the case study evidence.*" (2017).

6.05   The Chart Shows Recent Trends in Housing Prices

Chart 10 – Rent Trends in Miami

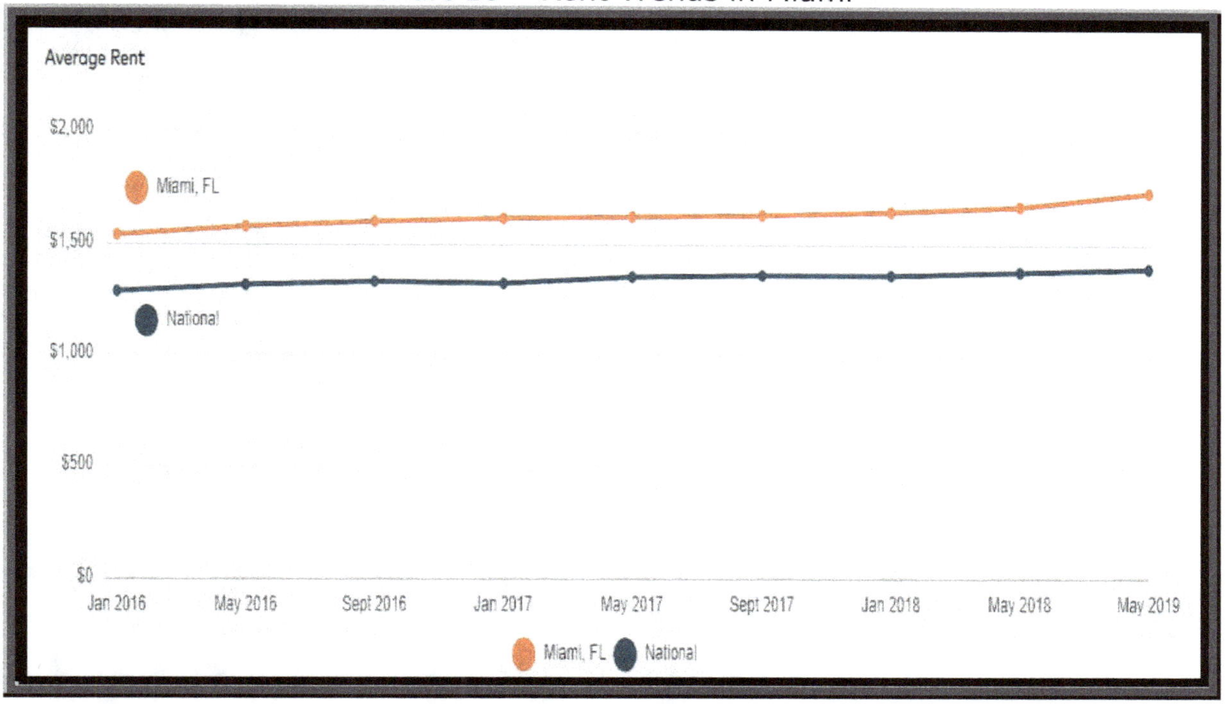

RENTCafé (2019). [82]

---

[82] Miami, FL Rental Market Trends. *"Average Rent in Miami & Rent Prices by Neighborhood."* RENTCafé. (2019).

Chapter 7

7.01 Affordable Housing by the Financial Institutions

From the evaluation conducted, it is clear that banks can play an active and essential role in mitigating the dilemma of homelessness, not only in the Miami-Dade area but also in the boarding communities of the local region as well. Different scholars have argued that the availability of affordable housing is a problem affecting many countries, regardless of their level of economic growth (MacKenzie, McNelis, Flatau, Valentine, & Seivwright. 2017). The issues associated with homelessness are getting much more severe in the United States, although it is one of the most developed countries in the world.

The disproportionate cost of living is one of the critical factors that is increasing the problem of homelessness in Miami and abroad. Where many families fail to prioritize shelter as their primary need; but instead dedicate their small income towards other essential basic needs such as food, water, clothing, and medicines for supporting themselves and their families. The financial institutions are vital for promoting economic development by encouraging subscribers to save money for shaping their future (Canepa & Khaled, 2018).[83] Banking members have the chance to access housing loans with their savings as security, which eventually helps in reducing the overall homelessness issue.

7.02 Mortgage Loans Provided at Low-Interest Rates

In the late 20th century, there has been an increase in demand for mortgage loans, which has become a central core facility provided by financial institutions (Schwartz, 2015).[84] Other agencies concerned have also tried to negotiate for low-interest rates to make the loans more accessible to those who require borrowing money for a home. The government can also provide tax incentives to both the loan providers and borrowers to increase the borrowing rate. The banks are mandated to monitor the usage of the loan facility to minimize the non-performing loans.

Canepa and Khaled (2018, p.3) posted that "credit risk" is closely related to the real estate market. Thus, implying that banks can use the real estate market in assessing the credit risk associated with borrowing. There is a high perceived dependence on this market by the banking products and services. The fluctuations in the housing prices can compromise the quality of assets of the banks and hence influencing their profitability more adversely as with their non-income producing list.

---

[83] A. Canepa. *"Housing, Housing Finance, and Credit Risk."* International Journal of Financial Studies. (2018).

[84] A. Schwartz. *Housing Policy in the United States*. NY.NY: Routledge (2015).

7.03   Canada's Unique Solution to Property Values

Access to affordable housing has become a common challenge in all countries and, most notably, in developing and underdeveloped countries. In 2016, while dealing with one of the difficulties of the housing market in Vancouver, Canada, had a growing issue of increased property values. Vancouver noticed that they had a considerable number of foreign investors, mostly from China. Chinese investors were buying properties at an alarming rate, which was prohibiting many low-income buyers from purchasing those types of properties (Nelson, 2018).[85]

7.04   The Average Cost and Definition of a Detached Home

In 2016, the average price for a "Detached Home" in Vancouver, had been valued at around C$1.56m (1.2 Million US Dollars). Vancouver's government's unique approach was to impose a 15% tax on foreign home buyers (Kassam, 2016).[86]

According to Business Dictionary (2019),[87]

> "A term used in real estate transactions to define a residential unit that shares no common walls with another house or dwelling. A detached home is a permanent dwelling, usually set on a separate lot and includes ownership rights to the land on which it is situated. A detached home is almost always considered a single-family home, meaning all internal areas are shared and in common. Also called single detached dwelling."

7.05   Imposing an International Buyers Tax

With Canada imposing this tax on international buyers, the yearly change in house prices declined from 35% down to about 10%, in the last 18 months; the market has been steadily rising :

> "Data from the provincial finance ministry suggests that only around 3.1% of real estate purchases in Vancouver in recent months went to buyers who weren't Canadian citizens, permanent residents, or didn't have work permits" (Nelson, 2018).[88]

---

[85] E, Nelson. "In the struggle to get housing market under control, Vancouver targets Chinese buyers." Quartz. (2018).
[86] A, Kassam. "Vancouver slaps 15% tax on foreign hose buyers in effort to cool market." The Guardian. (2016).
[87] Business Dictionary. "What is detached? Definition and Meaning." Business Directory. (2019).
[88] E. Nelson. "In the struggle to get its red-hot housing market under control, Vancouver targets Chinese buyers." Quartz. (2018).

Chapter 8

8.01   The Roles Banks can Play in Reducing Homelessness

According to the article published by Rojc (2017) [89], the banks have been actively participating in community development projects by providing grants to finance various projects, improving the well-being of the public. A good example is with the Bank of America's Charitable Foundation, which has continued to support programs on affordable housing initiatives. The bank is making significant grants for urban development programs. Different parties are looking forward to financing affordable housing projects in partnership with those in the private sectors and the local government, thus making The Home GAP Initiative a perfect opportunity for investors.

8.02   Banks and Lending Institutions Gifting Homes

to the Miami-Dade Government

Banks have been on the frontline in supporting projects in various cities across the nation. It invests in multiple programs that aim at financing the long-term affordability of housing projects. Adopting a gifting home program in Miami-Dade or abroad would be an effective way of providing for a more long-term permanent solution to the problem of homelessness and poverty by banks or lending institutions in gifting their non-income producing homes to The Home GAP Initiative.

8.03   Banking Sector Providing Incentives to Citizens

A report by Toepfer (2000)[90] revealed how banks could be in the frontline in addressing the housing challenges for people living in poverty. The article uses an example of the Grameen Bank of Bangladesh, which is known for its initiatives for housing homeless people through its lending policies that allow people to borrow without collateral. The system is mainly targeting the most impoverished individuals who do not own land but focuses on assisting them on how to secure some for borrowing. The bank ensures that the loan facility works with anyone who needs shelter but has no adequate financial resources. The loan has no standard conditions; only that the beneficiaries must be members with Grameen Bank for at least one year.

---

[89] P. Rojc. *"A bank looks to move the needle on affordable housing."* Inside Philanthropy. (2017).
[90] K. Toepfer. *"Strategies to combat Homelessness."* Nairobi: United Nations Centre for Human Settlements (Habitat). (2000).

8.04   Direct Bank Involvements in Real Estate

Grameen Bank has set in place strategies to make sure that the borrowers are utilizing the funds effectively. For instance, the bank requires the mortgagor to report to the bank every week to assess how they are using their loans accurately. The institution has also designed a plan that puts into account the needs of the target population. It helps in ensuring that the basic dwelling design is economical enough to be affordable by low-income individuals, especially from those living in rural areas. The plan should be strong and durable to minimize replacement costs. Also, the strategy must be comfortable enough to improve the well-being and self-image of the people with whom they are working with (Toepfer, 2000).

8.05   Provision for Options for Helping the Homeless

The issue of homelessness in the United States has been among the primary goals of political leaders. President Bush promoted a program known as the "Ten Year Plan to End Chronic Homelessness" (Poppe, 2015).[91] Also, there was the establishment of various housing policies rules and regulations, such as the American Recovery and Reinvestment Act, signed on February 17, 2009, called the Homelessness Prevention and Rapid Re-Housing Program (HPRP), for preventing the problem of homelessness (Cunningham & Batko, 2018). Also, the Obama Administration initiated and set a proposal in motion that was to effectively end veteran homelessness[92] by the end of 2016 (Obama, 2016). This goal was not achieved. These approaches appeared only to be effective in the short-term. It is ineffective as it has failed to provide a long-term solution to the problem of homelessness.

The significant rise in home prices has also acted as a major factor triggering the problem of homelessness in the United States. Due to the main level of inflation, the majority of the low-income earners have found it challenging to afford the basic needs for human survival. The low purchasing power of the consumers has also reduced and hereafter putting most people at risk of suffering from homelessness. Therefore, the initial step of reducing the problem of homelessness should start by bridging the gap between the rich and low-income (Hamidi et al., 2016).[93] Providing incentives and alternative loan recovery methods can also help in mitigating the risk and ensuring that low-income people have contractual access to housing loans (Pomeroy, 2014).[94]

---

[91] B. Poppe. *"The path forward: Rethinking the solutions for homelessness in Florida."* JP Morgan Chase & Co. (2015).
[92] President Obama, "Remarks at the Veterans Day Ceremony, Arlington Virginia, November 11, 2016.
[93] S. Hamidi. *"How affordable is HUD affordable housing?"* Routledge Taylor & Francis Group. (2016).
[94] S. Pomeroy. *"A literature review on approaches to end family homelessness."* Focus Consulting, Inc. (2014).

According to Alvarez and Montgomery (2019)[95], adopting The Home GAP Initiative of the banks donating homes to the homeless might be the best opportunity available, thereby aiding homeless individuals in Miami-Dade by housing 365 homeless people each year within the ten-year plan of this (future) sanctioned Home GAP Initiative by Miami-Dade County. A ten to twenty-year span can reduce the original homeless number of 3,839 homeless individuals residing in Miami-Dade to below 191 people. Nevertheless, after the initial completion of The Home GAP Initiative, the county will be in a position of generating a profit from what was once known as non-income producing properties. Those individuals who participated successfully in The Home GAP Initiative are now homeowners. The county will now receive property tax revenues of about $1,228,480.00 starting from the eleventh year, plus an additional savings of $44,678,282.00 that are now being paid out in aiding the Miami-Dade homeless population (see the Cost-Benefit Analysis Data Sheet in Appendix A).[96] The Home GAP Initiative – "Project 3" indicates that this is the most practical program and hence recommended for implementation as a suitable solution to the homelessness problem.

Chapter 9

9.01   Basic Shelter is a Need for Bridging the Gap

The shelter is one of the basic needs that every person ought to have for sustaining life. Thus, the acts of local banks participating in the providing of affordable housing are essential for a society to raise the living standards for the people within the community. Housing the homeless is seen as a significant investment that promotes public health (Bamberger, 2017).[97] According to the United Nations' report, Grameen Bank had produced about 305,600 dwellings by October 1994 (Toepfer, 2000). Miami-Dade has numerous banks within the county boundaries. Moreover, if these banks can adopt similar strategies, then these added solutions can be found in dealing with the problem of people living with no home.

As the low-income population increases in developing countries and within our own, due to low income and fluctuating levels of unemployment increases, the stakeholders concerned must continually find the best solutions to the challenges facing them and ensuring the provision for proper accommodations. By using this method, this will provide Miami-Dade into boosting their productivity and will increase the GDP per capita.

9.02   Bridging the Gap for the Homeless

Reducing the homeless problem in this country is highly dependent on the micro- and macro-economic performance of any housing programs. There is a high rate of disparity with the current housing scheme that requires the intervention of various parties. This will involve improving the living standards of every citizen and bridging the gap existing between the low-income or no-income and those who are financially well off. From the global perspective, there is existing pressure intended to deregulate the financial sectors in the attempts to increase the participation of the private sector for investing in the housing system.

---

[97] J. Bamberger. *"Reducing Homelessness by Embracing Housing as a Medicaid Benefit."* JAMA. (2016).

Hamidi, Ewing, and Renne (2016) [98] discussed that most of the individuals in low-income communities have difficulty accessing affordable housing loans. This is usually due to a lack of assets that can be generally utilized as collateral to secure their borrowing. From Toepfer (2000), [99] as shown by the Grameen Bank program, private sector investment in low-income communities can produce tangible results for all stakeholders. Banks in the US could implement similar approaches to those used by Grameen Bank.

The low- or no-income individuals cannot be put into a position of hardship and being discriminated against when the issuance of loan financing becomes available to them. That is, funds meant for accommodation should be possible for every person regardless of their ability to own security assets.

The resources available should be well-utilized to prevent families in any community from falling into homelessness (Ullman, 2016).[100] The project under consideration, in this case, The Home GAP Initiative, is to have participating banks donate from their non-income producing list of homes to Miami-Dade for those of low- or no-income households through this county-sanctioned approved program. In return, the county will give specific tax incentives to the banks or lending institutions participating in this program. Considering the significant investment that is required from private sector banks, favorable tax credits are a necessary tool to ensure engagement in The Home GAP Program Initiative. By increasing homeownership rates, the county will expand its tax base.

[98] S. Hamidi. *"How affordable is HUD affordable housing?"* Routledge Taylor & Francis Group. (2016).
[99] K. Toepfer. "Strategies to combat Homelessness." Nairobi: United Nations Centre for Human Settlements (Habitat, 2000).
[100] Ullman. "STATE OF FLORIDA REPORT: 2016 Homeless Census Estimates and Funding Need to End Chronic Homelessness.

Chapter 10

10.01 Banks Gifting Homes to Local Governments

Montgomery's (2019, p.12) study found that:

> *"Project 3 would get local participating banks to donate homes from their non-income producing list; to give homes to the homeless. Banks would be able to reduce their tax liability debt through a specific program designed by Miami-Dade County. Therefore, the costs or the acquisition of housing and land provided by banks would not have any out-of-pocket expenses for the county. The program is supervised by professionals, such as social workers and counselors who have been appropriately trained in a program for the county to ensure that homeless people are given homes. Gifting individual homes through this giveaway program will reduce the expenditures that Miami-Dade County will spend over this ten-year project. With Program 3, in taking care of the homeless, Miami-Dade would reduce their spending respectively with $44,678,282 in year eleven, $35,742,625.60 in year twelve, $26,806,969.20 in year thirteen, $17,871,312.80 in year fourteen, $8,935,656.40 in year fifteen, and nearly no costs in the sixteenth year and beyond."*

10.02 The Calculations Used to Evaluate Project 3 as the Best Policy Evaluation.

Chart 11 - Equations used to calculate NPV

$$Equation\ (1)\ Net\ Present\ Value = Present\ value\ of\ Benefits - Initial\ Cost\ of\ the\ Project$$

$$Equation\ (2)\ Project's\ Benefit\ Cost\ Ratio = \frac{Total\ Project\ Benefits}{Total\ Project\ Costs}$$

Equations used to calculate NPV (Montgomery, 2019). [101]

[101] Copyright Statement - From "Reducing Homelessness in Miami-Dade County," by J. Michael Montgomery: Unpublished manuscript from Florida International University. Copyright 2019. Adapted with permission.

10.03   Banks' Disposal of Unclaimed Lands

Banks can dispose of the unclaimed or abandoned assets to help the needy, including the lands and properties that will help in reducing the problem of homelessness (Samuels, 2016).[102] Most banks in this country possess plenty of homes that are underutilized or deemed as a non-income producing asset. The recommendation is that these homes should be donated to the less fortunate through The Home GAP Initiative to give homeless individuals access to affordable housing facilities. This act would be seen as a corporate social responsibility activity, which is vitally crucial in creating a competitive advantage.

The expenditure used for housing the homeless individuals could be allowable as a tax incentive, and hence, the programs help in minimizing the banks' tax liability. Such incentives are dedicated to ensuring that banks are investing more in activities that will promote economic development. Thus, it confirms that attempts at reducing homelessness are highly dependent on government intervention (Wheelock, 2006).[103] It can be achieved by either offering direct subsidies or tax incentives on various programs such as housing allowances, mortgage interest, public housing, and home giveaway programs, among others. These programs will improve the level of efficiency in the housing market levels and increase the supply to fill the gap existing that results in the shortage in this sector (U.S. Department of HUD - Office of Policy Development and Research, 2013).[104]

However, even the banks cannot provide a proper solution to the problem without the support from the government. The agencies concerned have to advocate for the adoption of effective strategies for addressing the issues of homelessness.

---

[102] A. Samuels. *"How can the US end homelessness?"* The Atlantic. (2016).
[103] D. Wheelock. *"What happens to banks when house prices fall? US Regional Housing Busts of the 80s and 90s."* (2006).
[104] U.S. Department of Housing and Urban Development Office of Policy Development and Research. *Strategies for improving homeless people's access to mainstream benefits and services.* US Department of HUD. (2013).

10.04   Government Providing Support for Banks

Schwartz (2015)[105] argues that housing is costly, and owning a home is dependent on the borrowed funds. The National Debt today (2019) is at $22 trillion and climbing, and according to Schwartz, residential mortgages in the US amounted to $10.7 trillion in 2013, and as of December 2018 is at $10.3 trillion indicating a slight downward trend. The residential mortgages in the US are equivalent to 46.8% of our national debts.

The local government of Miami-Dade should work collaboratively with all banks and financial institutions to provide incentives. Thus the idea of encouraging any banking participants in focusing their home gifting efforts and participation in The Home GAP Initiative to aid in the reduction of the problem of homelessness. Appropriate rules and regulations should provide for high efficiency in housing the homeless populace for this program. Various scholars have advocated for the need to create affordable housing programs and avoid much focus on short-term goals; however, instead, focus on providing long-term solutions as does with the proposed Home GAP Initiative.

---

[105] A. Schwartz. *"Housing policy in the United States (3rd edition)."* NY, NY: Routledge. (2015).

Chapter 11

11.01   Finland's PAAVO Programme

Gives Homes to the Homeless

Finland's government uses a home giveaway program called PAAVO[106] "The National Programme to End Long-term Homelessness," and it is working. Their approach is simple; one cannot have permanent, stable housing without having a home in the first place. Finland is just one of the fewest countries that have reduced the numbers in its homeless population. Since its initiation, the number of homeless people has dropped from around 3,600 people in 2008, down to 2,000 people in 2016 (Foster, 2017).

PAAVO is a long-term program that has been established for more than ten years. Finland's government purchases housing units from the private market. These purchases have been a critical factor in reducing the homeless population and also play a factor in the prevention of those people returning to a homeless status. The program gives those individuals a stable environment that allows them to take care of their mental health and medical needs and to put themselves into a position of finding a job and having a steady income in which to deal with their situation. Motivation is crucial to those homeless individuals who have been afforded the opportunity of obtaining these homes to do what they must do to keep that home.

Chart 12 – PAAVO Homelessness Statistics

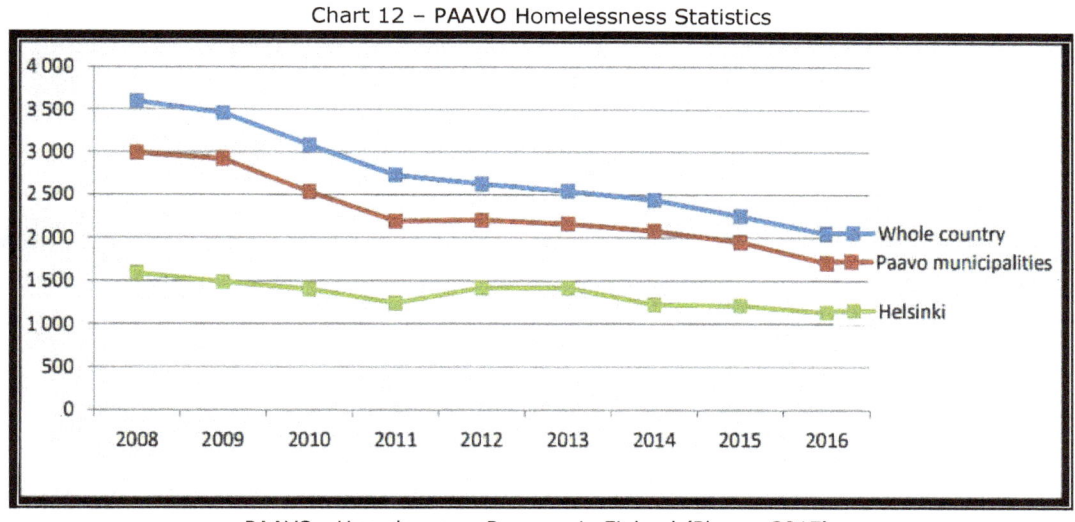

PAAVO - Homelessness Program in Finland (Pleace, 2017).

---

[106] J. Kaakinen. "*How Finland is tackling homelessness.*" World Economic Forum. (2019).

PAAVO was a two-stage program, with Stage 1 starting in 2008, and then Stage 2 was completed by 2011 (Pleace, 2017).[107]

> "Paavo I, the first stage of the integrated Finnish national homelessness strategy, was launched in 2008, with the goal of halving the level of long-term homelessness by 2011. The Paavo I strategy was designed to deliver 1,250 new dwellings and supported housing units in 10 cities, replacing emergency shelters and communal services with supported housing units that offered permanent tenancies. As has been noted elsewhere, Paavo I was distinguished as much by the political acumen with which the strategy was orchestrated, the bringing together all levels of government, quasi-governmental agencies and the homelessness sector, as it was by the adoption of a Housing First model."

The Home Giveaway Program Initiative is a similar concept to that of The PAAVO Action Plan. The difference is that the local banking industry will be gifting homes from their "non-income producing list" to any government entity in exchange for specific tax incentives to be determined. This program would allow most governments not to have any additional expenditures of purchasing homes for The Home Giveaway Program. Modeling Finland's Action Plan would be an added solution for any city having a homeless program to transition into for the end goal of reducing homelessness in their region.

---

[107] N. Pleace. "*The Action Plan for Preventing Homelessness in Finland 2016-2019: The Culmination of an Integrated Strategy to End Homelessness?*" University of York. (2017).

Chapter 12

12.01   Review of the Literature Homelessness Issues [108]

Today, too many people are living on the streets of the United States without any shelter. This societal issue is often disregarded and deemed inconsequential. Homelessness consists of different types of people, men, women, children, and to include all groups of racial and ethnic backgrounds. Every homeless person's situation is different. These individuals may have financial difficulties, they may come from a domestic violence situation, they may even have mental issues that are making their conditions difficult, and that leads them to become homeless. Homeless people found in this type of situation often face the embarrassment of ridicule and stereotypes that are unfounded, further exacerbating a homeless person's daily living.

[109] Homelessness since 2013 has increased significantly, with approximately five states housing more than half of the homeless population. One of these states is Florida, which is focused on temporary solutions to better combat chronic homelessness across the region. The main findings from their census had determined that an overconcentration of homeless individuals saw an increase at the rate between 11% and 20%. The data was extracted from federal government records on their census with the given year. The author mentioned that slight improvement had been made in some areas, but more progress and collaboration are needed to breakeven the rate of growth. The author inferred that a more significant investment is to be made if the crisis would end, adding to the validity to establish a long-term solution.

[110]Outside of the United States, the Housing First initiative in Canada has taken an approach that collaboratively uses caring principles to reduce the amount of homelessness in the country. This program is the closest variation to a long-term plan for the sustainability of homeless individuals to transition from a homelessness status to being an adequate and productive citizen. The main findings through the creation of this initiative that used agency records and semi-structured interviews. This suggests that little government intervention is needed to foster community engagement to assist homeless individuals in finding a home for themselves and agree to monthly check-ups. As a broad program, it contains characteristics of what Home GAP would be inheriting, but tenant rights come with conditions outlined in the Home GAP Initiative.

---

[108] Copyright Statement - From "Public Evaluation Design for Miami-Dade Home GAP," by J. Michael Montgomery and Sandro Alvarez, 2019: Unpublished manuscript. *Florida International University.* Adapted with permission.
[109] Covert, B. (2013). More Than 600,000 Americans Are Homeless On Any Given Night. *Think Progress.*
[110] Government of Canada, (2019). Housing First. *Government of Canada.*

[111]A community initiative in Kansas resulted in the construction of twenty-five homes for homeless veterans. The homes are a long-term sustainability plan which takes the form of permanent housing. Leadership was the main factor in making the project happen for homeless veterans, regardless of discharge status. Interviews taken from individuals after the construction of these homes resulted in high levels of satisfaction in having a home that was built with a foundation and funded by the community. In the United States, this project is significant in that it also takes the idea of having a solution for chronic homelessness, but the restrictions are only for the veterans. The author concurred that it is a step in the correct direction in one of the many solutions that can be used to combat homelessness in the United States. The author presents an idea that can be translated to Miami-Dade County, where instead of building homes, can utilize those non-income producing assets.

[112]One of the critical items to Home GAP becoming a successful project is the integration of licensed clinical social workers to work with homeless individuals in following a series of tasks to bring about a transition back into a productive urban life. Treatment plans can include attending individual vocational workshops, developing personal goals, requiring to complete specific actions that are to their best interest, and meeting with a social worker to discuss the progress of the individual. Data from surveys display an analysis that treatment plans are effective in tackling challenges that homeless individuals can face, with each plan being catered to specific needs. Being that the Home GAP program's main item for success is the implementation of social workers throughout each phase of this theoretical program. In turn, social workers develop treatment plans for these homeless individuals, binds together productivity, and the reward of being granted the title of a home by Miami-Dade county.

[113]The author displays critical data concerning the usage of drugs and alcohol on the homeless population - up to 40% of all homeless individuals are affected in this criterion. The analysis of the findings indicates the importance of addressing the concern directly through working with them to the dangers of using risky substances at a sensitive time in their lives. By engaging in the activities, other mental health concerns can arise from the usage, such as manic episodes or depression. Being that the Home GAP theoretical program aims to address potentials of drug or alcohol usage throughout the treatment plan of need, the author emphasizes the drastic assistance in implementing a design that is both beneficial to the homeless individuals but recognizes the importance of seeking other alternatives instead of drugs or alcohol.

[114]Code of Federal Regulations (n.d.) entails various concepts of code of federal regulations (CFR), a codification of the permanent and general rules and regulations, the administrative laws. This includes the definition of what is considered a non-income producing assets by all banks and lending institutions. The CFR website aims to help people understand some of the broad areas that are subject to federal law. CFR is divided into various volumes, which are updated regularly — published by the federal register as per executive departments and government agencies. It is a single publication that presents a complete text of regulatory agencies. Each chapter of the publications covers specific areas of regulatory concepts in the United States.

---

[111] Lounsberry, S. (2018). Planned Longmont tiny home village will give 25 homeless veterans free temporary housing. *University Wire.*
[112] VHA Office of Mental Health. (2012). Homeless Veterans. *Veterans Admin.*
[113] McCarty, D., Argeriou, M., Huebner, R. B., & Lubran, B. (1991). Alcoholism, drug abuse, and the homeless. *American Psychologist, 46(11), 1139-1148.*
[114] Code of Federal Regulations (n.d.). *Archives.Gov.*

[115]Broward Outreach Center (2019) has been serving homeless individuals in Miami and Broward County since 1922 and is a division of the Miami Rescue Mission (MRM). The material explores some of the activities conducted in Miami to help homeless people, and it focuses on the establishments that have been put in place to allow workers and volunteers to help the needy within the community. MRM aims to encourage people to volunteer and helps those in need and their practices are primarily focused on providing basic needs for these people that are needy or homeless in the community, which involves providing resources to them, such as meals, finding employment, and housing for men, women, and children.

[116]Miami-Dade County Homeless Trust (Mozloom,2019) reports on the homeless population in Miami-Dade. The commentary focusses on homeless people in Miami-Dade County. A survey is conducted to gather data on homeless people, and the results show that there was a drop in the amount of homeless people from previous years and discusses the changes that have occurred based on the societal situation. Point-in-Time (PIT) is the method used to gauge the efficiency of the programs established to end homelessness.

These surveys identify the unsheltered individuals and the challenges they are facing. Some issues individuals face are mental health, disabilities, and abuse of substances. The PIT survey count is utilized within the county to establish the geographic and lifestyle analyses concerning homeless people.

[117]The MintPress News Desk, (2015) material report is about people experiencing homelessness. In Miami-Dade, there are many people without a place to live; most of them are alone living on the streets. However, the homeless situation is still quite evident. The material identifies programs that have been established to attempt to end homelessness and decrease the number of homeless individuals. The report identifies the financial stressors concerning the banks and their contribution to the foreclosure of identified homes. Foreclosure of several homes is one of the leading causes of homelessness. Despite a high number of homeless individuals living on the streets, the material identifies that there is some decrease in the cases of homelessness. Data from the National Alliance to End Homeless is used for the analysis trends.

[118]The article "Bringing it All Together: Integrating Services to Address Homelessness" (Turner 2019) explores some of the services that attempt to end the societal issue of homelessness. Through the Master of Social Work (MSW), the system aims to establish and address this issue to ensure that the number of homeless people reduces in numbers. Some of the efforts to resolve this issue lead to additional complexities within the population. Findings affirm that as the initiatives to address this matter remain essential, they cannot serve as the panacea to homelessness and other social challenges. The government, service providers, and the sponsors have increasingly facilitated the initiatives to attempt to end homelessness. The systems, policies, and processes are used to maximize the resources available to help resolve this matter of the homelessness issue.

[115] Broward Outreach Center (2019). Serving People Experiencing Homelessness of Miami and Broward Since 1922. *A Division of Miami Rescue Mission.*
[116] Mozloom, L. (2019). *Miami-Dade County Homeless Trust reports homelessness in Miami-Dade is at a record low.* Miami-Dade County.
[117] MintPress News Desk. Empty Homes Outnumber The Homeless 6 to 1, So Why Not Give Them Homes? *Mintpress News.* (2015).
[118] Turner, A. (2019). Bringing it All Together: Integrating Services to Address Homelessness. *SSRN.*

Chart 13 – Theoretical Perspective and Literature Review

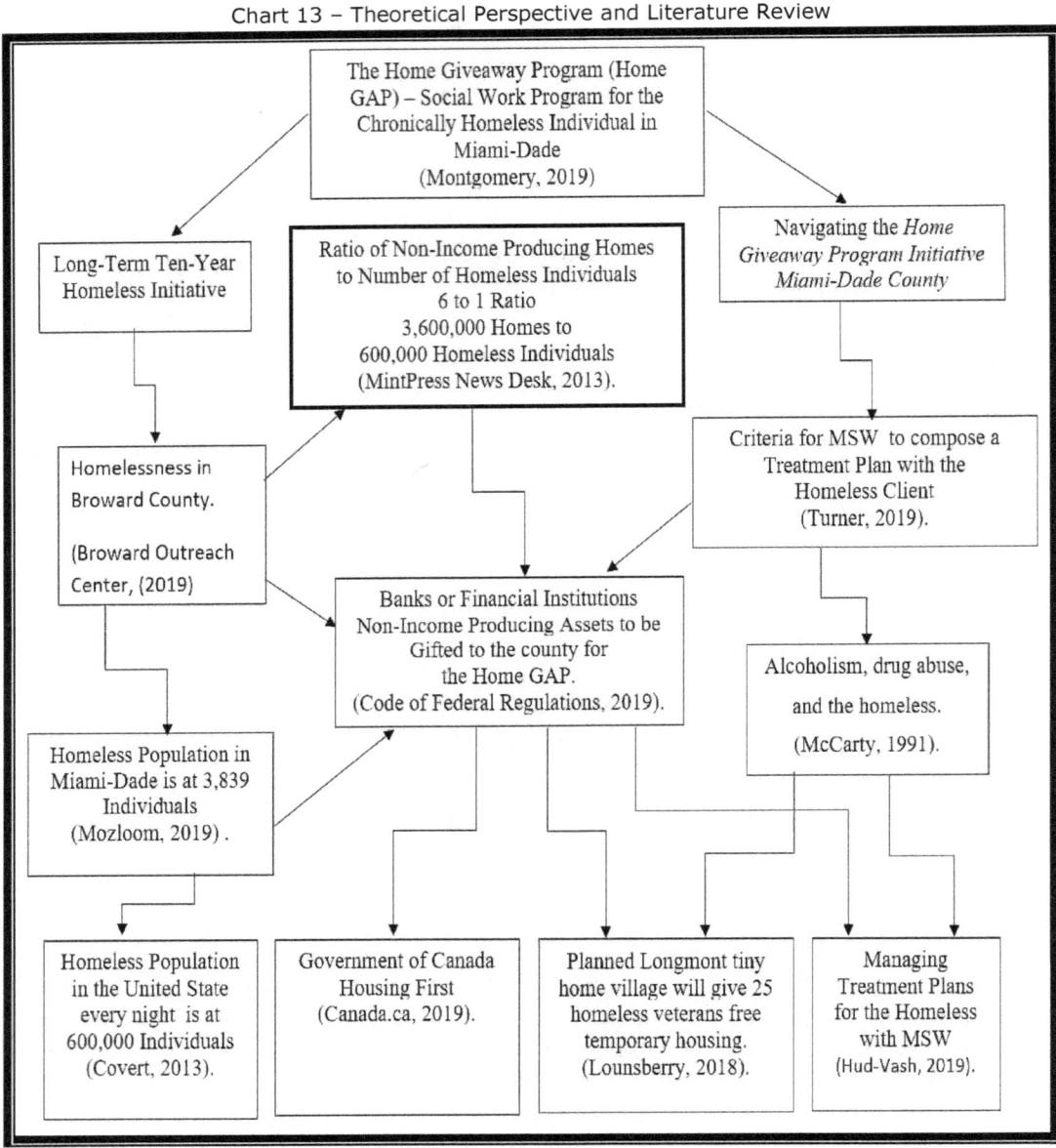

Literature Review Flowchart (Montgomery & Alvarez, 2019).

12.03   Data Collection [120]

The indicators integrate quality and quantity. Quantity from the amount of non-income producing homes and the number of treatment plans approved, to the enhancement of financial knowledge and personal development. They are critical indicators combined for program success. This information will be collected through agency records as it will be the government's program. The survey is conducted in-person as a mandatory requirement as the final item before having the home's title granted. Therefore, this method eliminates all complications with a lack of survey responses and reflects their experience with the program. The sample size will consist of those who have reached the 10-year mark and optional if unsuccessful. The only limitation would be the refusal to take the survey. Survey follows a seven-point Likert scale, the same scale used in Broward Outreach and HUD-Vash.

12.04   Review of Related Literature

Today, in the United States, homelessness remains a reality in society as it is still at a rise. Whether it is in the streets, parks, cities, restaurant pathways, one is likely to encounter a homeless individual. For a while now, the government has made different short-term attempts to eradicate the problem on most levels; however, comprehensive programs to address the issue have proven elusive. According to an article by Semuels (2018), he evaluates different questions on the effectiveness of long-term solutions in completely eradicating homelessness. The first action to address homelessness is increasing the number of shelters and ensure that they are available for the homeless. Over time, the United States government has given homeless individuals tents; however, is this a feasible solution? According to Semuels (2018), emergency shelters cost an average of $4,819 monthly, while a housing voucher is $1,162. Such incidences raise issues on the effectiveness of short-term solutions to eradicate homelessness. The affordability of housing is an ultimate solution to address homelessness as it offers access to other fundamental services.

However, issues like job loss, disability, poverty, drug abuse, mental or health issues, abusive homes, eviction, and immigration have resulted in the high levels of homelessness in Miami-Dade and other cities all over the world. According to the article by Trauschke (2019), the surveyor identified approximately 804 homeless individuals across North Central Florida counties as of January 2019. The figure represents a 6% increase from 2018. With such issues on immigration, this is likely to affect the long-term solutions to homelessness than the short-term solution. Often, immigration begins as a small issue, which later escalates, changing the social and economic structure. If not handled as expected by the United States, this results in a higher number of homeless individuals.

According to Minnery and Greenhalgh's (2007) study, their report looks at providing some of the approaches that could reduce homelessness across the United States and other countries. For instance, the Australian government has adopted the Supported Accommodation Assistance Program (SAAP) as a national approach to counter homelessness. In the eradication of homelessness, workable and effective policies should be developed based on the precise definition of homelessness. By presenting new strategies in Australia, European Union, and the United States, this article indicates that homelessness should be perceived as a lively action that could include moving in and out of houses, among added support services. Through good policies, they help address the social, psychological, and housing needs of homeless individuals and enhance independence.

Moreover, Poppe (2015) sets out to investigate the causes of homelessness in Florida, community response, and identify the various opportunities for setting programs that offer tangible solutions for homeless individuals. Based on a 2014 Annual Homeless Assessment Report, it provides that approximately 41,000 people suffer homelessness in Florida daily. [121]

Even though addressing homelessness is a bipartisan objective, the federal government cannot work alone to resolve the issue. The states must be engaged to establish proper reforms and policy changes. The implementation of Housing First frameworks is likely to help end the growing concern and reduce cost as the case in Utah. According to Poppe (2015), 3.2 million households, 45% of the total homes, are struggling to have enough money for various necessities like food, healthcare, housing, and basic necessities such as soap, toothpaste, and toilet paper. Also, there is a 7% increase in chronic homelessness. As such, initiatives to end homelessness should look beyond temporary relief in a handout, and focus on ways to end poverty.

12.05   Scope and Limitations

With the different causes of homelessness among people in Miami-Dade County, the United States, and across the world, there is no single approach that addresses all the reasons for being homeless. Through the short-term solution, it would only mean that not all the individuals would be considered and that the problem would likely occur again. However, with long-term solutions, it means that the chances of addressing more causes and populations are higher while at the same time, ensuring that the problems of the homelessness are close to becoming permanently eradicated.

As a limitation to the study, it is difficult to establish the actual number of homeless individuals. In most of the cases, the real numbers happen to be between two to ten times the provided estimate. As a result, this transpired to other limitations such as difficulty in determining necessary resources, and the possibility of frauds where cost is involved.

---

[121] B. Poppe. *"The path forward: Rethinking the solutions for homelessness in Florida."* JP Morgan Chase & Co. (2015).

12.06   Background of the Study

Extensive research has been undertaken on homelessness in the US, especially in Miami-Dade County. People who are experiencing homelessness have been referred to as "homeless identity." There is no universal description of what a homeless identity and homelessness are, but when the two terms pop up, there is this mental picture of people sleeping in boxes in the street. These people are often described as being dirty and having a duffel coat.

Homelessness is a severe problem around the world that causes pain to the victims and costs governments much money in efforts to help the homeless. World Health Organization recommends job creation and an increase in the minimum wage. Ullman (2016) documents a census on the homeless population in the US, showing that the homeless population does not lean on a particular group, but rather it is diverse. The homeless are comprised of adult males, adult females, children, and families (Whitbeck, 2017). Hirschkorn (2012) writes that there are sixteen thousand homeless people in Tampa Bay. From the findings of Ullman (2016), the homeless people in the county of Miami-Dade as of 2016 were approximately 3,839.

According to recent findings, Miami-Dade showed that the number has reduced to 3,526 in 2019 (Mozloom, 2019), showing that about 320 people had found solutions to homelessness. Barszewski (2018) also writes that if the gaps in the solutions sourced are addressed, the homeless population can drop. Barszewski shows the figures of people who had found solutions to homelessness in Broward County, Florida. The numbers in some counties like Putnam County, Florida, have remained the same (Trauschke, 2019). As by the figure presented by Ullman (2016), Miami-Dade was spending more than $12,000 per person to take care of homeless people. Annually, this cost amounts to $44,678,282.00.

However, The Home Giveaway Program Initiative seeks not only to provide homes for the homeless but also to educate them on how to become stable, responsible, and productive citizens. Individuals that participate in the program would generate property rental revenues and property tax revenues for county stakeholders (Montgomery, 2019).

12.07   Presentation and Analysis of the Data

In the issue of homelessness, it is essential to note that examining the numbers is necessary since it provides the different populations and resources required to address a given community. According to Ullman (2016) on the National Homeless Information Project, of the estimated 31,030 homeless individuals in Florida, 5,302 are individuals suffering from chronic illness, 2,757 belong in a household, 2,543 are veterans, and 1,892 are young adults between the age of 18-24.

With a view in Florida on counties such as Broward, Pinellas, and Tampa, there are significantly different homeless populations. For instance, according to Barszewski (2018), Broward County has 2,318 homeless individuals, 1,588 of whom are male and 718 females while, Pinellas County has 11,843 homeless persons, 1,984 of which are households, and 1,214 are children (Moore, 2017). In Tampa, according to Hirschkorn (2012), has an estimated 16,000 people, where one in five are children (Hirschkorn, 2012). Moreover, Miami-Dade hosts 3,628 homeless people, where 35% of them were male, and 46% of them had a disability (Montgomery, 2019). With the given statistics, one can quickly evaluate the various changes in terms of homelessness and assess the needed actions to address the issue. Furthermore, they signify the need for proper housing first policies to help reduce homeless in Miami-Dade County and other locations (Mozloom, 2019).

Conclusion

The implementation of housing principles has been in the majority of cities and nations worldwide for many years to assist its inhabitants with adequate shelter. At times, when homelessness gets to be a significant issue, new and effective principled programs need to be established. These principles act as a way of fighting homelessness.[122]

These policy works are grounded on the hypothesis that the homelessness issue mitigated with the provision of shelters and emergency housings plays an adequate role in reducing these social issues. Social protection plays a significant part in the configuration of the displaced population in any country through the provision of access to appropriate social systems that are characterized by affordable access to health care and housing facilities. Also, a society that provides social support, including income security, unemployment, invalidity, or protection from loss of primary income, a permanent residence, can guarantee the reduction or non-occurrence of homelessness, as does with the implementation of this enterprise called: "The Home GAP Initiative."[123]

The analysis indicates that banks have a considerable influence on the efforts dedicated to reducing the problem of homelessness. The issue of homelessness has become more significant in the modern days, and therefore, it requires innovative strategies to be adopted for mitigating the consequences for all parties and stakeholders involved.

Banks and Lending Institutions can take various means when seeking for a long-term solution, then identifying the problem in addition to giving away homes from their non-income producing list to those individuals with low- or no-income. Several banks and lending institutions in any country could be enticed with specific tax incentives with their gift of donating houses to The Home GAP Initiative to the government for improving the living standards of the low- or no-income community.

The Home Giveaway Program Initiative (Home GAP) would be crucial in reducing the number of homeless low-income, and no-income earners in government-run homelessness programs in the US and abroad, as most people will have then have the opportunity to afford the rates that are being offered by government officials through "The Home GAP Initiative." Various rules and regulations set in place will be crucial in ensuring that "The Home GAP Initiative" is effectively implemented in any government-run homeless program for those individuals who are participating in this type of curriculum.

More specifically, these strategies are directed to the people living in poverty in the effort of ensuring that every person has been given equal opportunity in society regardless of their social status. Various stakeholders and agencies concerned must play their part in winning the war against the homelessness problem - not only in Miami-Dade, but also for the rest of the country, and the rest of the world.

---

[122] From "Homelessness Issues In Miami-Dade Florida," by J. Michael Montgomery: Unpublished manuscript Florida International University. Copyright 2019. Adapted with permission.

[123] Copyright Statement - From "Public Evaluation Design for Miami-Dade Home GAP," by J. Michael Montgomery and Sandro Alvarez, 2019: Unpublished manuscript. *Florida International University.* Adapted with permission.

Proper policies and procedures should be put in place to improve the quality of life for all residents to ensure a better future. Involving banks in the various Housing and Urban Development programs would help in yielding additional results in solving the issue of homelessness.

Semuels (2018) [124] writes many factors have led to increased levels of homelessness, the popular ones being insufficiencies of affordable housing, and the high poverty rate and remains a substantial issue in the US and other nations worldwide. The county of Miami-Dade in Florida is an example of a region that has the same problem with the 3,628 homeless people that cost the county millions in aid support. Previous methods to curb homelessness have been unfruitful since most of them have been short-term solutions resulting in a continuous cycle of homelessness. According to Moore (2017), most governments face the challenges of putting a focus on the social issue of homelessness. Moore (2017) claims that this fight for justice has proven to be a menace because the resources that are instrumental in combatting it are insufficient. It is mortifying for both an individual and a government to be considered homeless.

Nonetheless, a long-term solution would be efficient and essential to eradicate homelessness. The proposed "Home Giveaway Program Initiative" is useful since it warrants affordable housing for homeless individuals. Home GAP also has training programs that empower the homeless to become productive citizens. In The Home GAP Initiative, the homeless individual is supposed to agree in the participation of this long-term ten-year transformational strategy in which a social worker would arrange a treatment plan that will solely address the needs of the specific homeless person. When implemented for use, any government entity will be favoring a home to a perpetual inventory for The Home GAP Initiative, a system that will evolve over ten years.

A lot of monetary resources are expected to be used at the inception of this initiative. After some time, a winning result is expected from program participants; thus, they will now have a chance of owning a home and will get rehabilitated. For sustenance purposes, there will be paying of rent, and other property charge portions will be paid once a title is given to the recipient. Service and property charges will augment for every client who has proceeded onward from The Home GAP Initiative endeavor. The government will be gathering revenue from those homes that were once declared as a non-income producing asset. By executing The Home GAP Initiative, the remaining debt from the program will be at a breakeven point concerning the issue with the costs of managing desperate individuals out of homelessness. These utilizations will profoundly lessen, and the budget can realize higher open financing.[125]

Based on the research findings, a long-term solution to homelessness can be achieved and eradicate this chronic problem. The gaps in previous short-term solutions that have been used in the past; are what made them not to be as efficient. Since the effects of short-term solutions are susceptible to be affected by things like immigration and are not binding, The Home GAP Initiative is likely to address the issue to ensure affordable housing in the long-term.

The Home GAP Initiative[126] will have long-term beneficial gains to the Miami-Dade community would be a win-win situation for all. In Stage One of The Home GAP Initiative, it is designed with the focus on county-appointed officials to seek out all homeless individuals within Miami-Dade County; to include veterans regardless of their character of discharge. With the county spending $44,678,282.00 on 3,839 homeless people a year to take care of the basic needs of the homeless individuals (Ullman, 2016); [127] it is paramount for all stakeholders to ensure that all stages of The Home GAP Initiative be sufficient to obtain the result of eliminating the number of homeless individuals living on the street, to cut that rate down to 95% in twenty years.

The first intervention will come two years after the implementation of the Home GAP Initiative, followed by three more interventions according to the Interrupted Time Series schedule. The Home GAP Initiative is expected to reduce homelessness in Miami-Dade after the implementation of this unique program. Miami-Dade and all stakeholders will see the homelessness numbers of 3,839 individuals that are impacting the county in 2020 down to 191 homeless individuals by 2040.

The Home GAP Initiative is the best long-term solution with the most beneficial gains for those who are homeless, any government, community, and all stakeholders willing to propose and implement this "Win-Win" program for all involved.

---

[126] Copyright Statement - From "Public Evaluation Design for Miami-Dade Home GAP," by J. Michael Montgomery and Sandro Alvarez, 2019: Unpublished manuscript. *Florida International University.* Adapted with permission.
[127] Ullman. "STATE OF FLORIDA REPORT: 2016 Homeless Census Estimates and Funding Need to End Chronic Homelessness.

References

Admin (2009). Natural Disasters and Homelessness. *National Coalition for the Homeless.* Retrieved from https://nationalhomeless.org/wp-content/uploads/2017/09/Natural-Disasters-and-Homelessness-Fact-Sheet-2009.pdf

ASPE. (2019). U.S. Federal Poverty Guidelines Used to Determine Financial Eligibility for Certain Federal Programs. ASPE. Retrieved from https://aspe.hhs.gov/poverty-guidelines

Atuheire, K., & Karyeija, G. K. (2014). THE ROLE OF FINANCIAL INSTITUTIONS TOWARDS AFFORDABLE HOUSING TO URBAN MIDDLE INCOME EARNERS: EVIDENCE FROM KAMPALA CITY, UGANDA. *African Journal of Social Work, 4(2), 2014.* Retrieved from https://www.ajol.info/index.php/ajsw/article/viewFile/127533/117058

Bamberger, J. (2016). Reducing Homelessness by Embracing Housing as a Medicaid Benefit. *JAMA Internal Medicine.* Retrieved from https://jamanetwork.com/journals/jamainternalmedicine/article-abstract/2528294

Barszewski, L. (2018, May 7). *"Broward's homeless population drops, survey says."* Sun-Sentinel. Retrieved from https://www.sun-sentinel.com/local/broward/fl-sb-broward-homeless-count-drops-2018-story.html

Broward Outreach Center (2019). Serving People Experiencing Homelessness of Miami and Broward Since 1922. *A Division of Miami Rescue Mission.* Retrieved from http://www.browardoutreachcenter.org/

Business Dictionary. (n.d.). What is detached? Definition and meaning. *Business Directory.* Retrieved from http://www.businessdictionary.com/definition/detached.html

Canepa, A., & Khaled, F. (2018). Housing, Housing Finance, and Credit Risk. *International Journal of Financial Studies.* Retrieved from https://www.mdpi.com/2227-7072/6/2/50/htm

Carson, B. (n.d.). Homelessness Prevention and Rapid Re-Housing Program. *Hud Exchange, Info.* Retrieved from https://www.hudexchange.info/programs/hprp/

Chakraborty, B. (2019). San Francisco homeless stats soar: city blames
    big business, residents blame officials. *Fox News.* Retrieved from
    https://www.foxnews.com/us/san-francisco-homeless-stats-city-blames-big-business-residents-officials

Clemons, Randy, & McBeth, Mark. (2020). *Public Policy Praxis: a case
    approach for understanding policy and analysis*. ROUTLEDGE.

Clos, J. (2017). The New Urban Agenda. *Habitat3.* Retrieved from
    http://habitat3.org/wp-content/uploads/NUA-English.pdf

Code of Federal Regulations, Code of Federal Regulations (n.d.).
    Archives.Gov. Retrieved from https://www.archives.gov/federal-register/cfr

Covert, B. (2013). More Than 600,000 Americans Are Homeless On Any
    Given Night. *Think Progress.* Retrieved from https://archive.thinkprogress.org/more-than-600-000-americans-are-homeless-on-any-given-night-b0f7bddda987/

Cundiff, S. (2015). Veterans and Addictions: Homelessness and Post-
    Traumatic Stress Disorder.
    The Commonwealth of Kentucky. Retrieved from
    http://dbhdid.ky.gov/dbh/documents/ksaods/2015/Cundiff1.pdf?t=10344708232018

Cunningham, M., & Batko, S. (2018). Rapid Re-housing's Role in
    Responding to Homelessness. *Urban Institute.* Retrieved from
    https://www.urban.org/sites/default/files/publication/99153/rapid_re-housings_role_in_responding_to_homelessness_2.pdf

D'erasmo, P. (2019). Banking Trends: Estimating Todays Commercial
    Real Estate Risk. *Banking Trends.* Retrieved from https://philadelphiafed.org/-/media/research-and-data/publications/banking-trends/2019/bt-estimating-todays-commercial-real-estate-risk.pdf?la=en

Definition of Value of Non-Income Producing Assets. (n.d.). *Law Insider.*
    Retrieved from https://www.lawinsider.com/dictionary/value-of-non-income-producing-assets

Dietz, R. (2015). How Many People Have Benefitted from the Affordable Housing Credit? *NAHB. National Association of Home Builders.* Retrieved from http://eyeonhousing.org/2015/11/how-many-people-have-benefitted-from-the-affordable-housing-credit/

Florida International University site information. Retrieved from http://www.fiu.edu (2020).

Foster, D. (2017). How Finland solved homelessness | Interview: Juha Kaakinen. *The Guardian.* Retrieved from https://www.theguardian.com/housing-network/2017/mar/22/finland-solved-homelessness-eu-crisis-housing-first

Freddie Mac. (2017). Multifamily 2017 Outlook: Positioned for Further Growth. *Freddie Mac.* Retrieved from https://mf.freddiemac.com/research/outlook/20170207-2017-outlook.html

Galley, C. (2018). The Connection Between Homelessness, Immigration, and Displacement. *Center on Human Rights Education.* Retrieved from https://www.centeronhumanrightseducation.org/connection-homelessness-immigration-displacement/

George Lucas Quotes. (n.d.). Quotes.net. Retrieved April 13, 2020. From **https://www.quotes.net/authors/George+Lucas+Quotes**

Government of Canada, (2019). Housing First. *Government of Canada.* Retrieved from https://www.canada.ca/en/employment-social-development/programs/homelessness/resources/housing-first.html

Gregerson, A. (2013). Homelessness presents numerous problems for South Florida. *News Reporting and the Internet.* University of Miami, Coral Gables. Retrieved from https://www.coursehero.com/file/56298630/News-Reporting-and-the-Internetdocx/

Gross, S. J. (2019). How much vacant housing is there in Florida? You asked, we answered. *Miami Herald.* Retrieved from https://www.miamiherald.com/news/politics-government/influencers/article233627502.html

Hamidi, S., Ewing, R., & Renne, J. (2016). How Affordable Is HUD Affordable Housing? Housing Policy Debate, 26(3), 437–455. Taylor & Francis Online. Retrieved from https://www.tandfonline.com/doi/abs/10.1080/10511482.2015.1123753

Hirschkorn, P. (2012, August 26). "Tampa area has the nation's highest homelessness rate." *CBS Evening News*. Retrieved from https://www.cbsnews.com/news/tampa-area-has-nations-highest-homelessness-rate/

Home Advisor. (2019). How Much Does It Cost To Build A House? Home Advisor. Retrieved from https://www.homeadvisor.com/cost/architects-and-engineers/build-a-house/

Homelessness 101. (2019). The face of homelessness has changed. Homelessness 101. Coalition for the Homeless. Retrieved from https://nhsdc.org/wp-content/uploads/2019/05/1.1.A-Homelessness-101.pdf

Homeless Trust. (2019). Miami-Dade County Homeless Trust. Miami-Dade County. Retrieved from http://Homelesstrust.org

I Am Expat. (n.d.). Rental Security Deposits In The Netherlands. *IAMEXPAT*. Retrieved from https://www.iamexpat.nl/housing/netherlands-rentals/rental-security-deposit

Johnson, G., Parkinson, S., Tseng, Y., Kuehnle, D. (2019). Long-Term Homelessness: Understanding the Challenge – 12 Months Outcomes From the Journey to Social Inclusion Pilot Program. *SSRN. Elsevier*. Retrieved from https://papers.ssrn.com/sol3/papers.cfm?abstract_id=3476196

Johnson, Ribar, C., D., Zhu, & Anna. (2017). Women's Homelessness: International Evidence on Causes, Consequences, Coping, and Policies. *Elsevier Publishing Company*. Retrieved from https://papers.ssrn.com/sol3/papers.cfm?abstract_id=2927811

Kaakinen, J. (2019). How Finland is tackling homelessness. *World Economic Forum*. Retrieved from https://www.weforum.org/agenda/2019/04/how-finland-is-tackling-homelessness

Kassam, A. (2016). Vancouver slaps 15% tax on foreign house buyers in effort to cool market. *The Guardian*. Retrieved from https://www.theguardian.com/world/2016/aug/02/vancouver-real-estate-foreign-house-buyers-tax

King, S. (2019). Kansas City Tiny-House Village For Veterans Is A Model For Other Cities, Hartzler Says. *KCUR*. Retrieved from https://www.kcur.org/post/kansas-city-tiny-house-village-veterans-model-other-cities-hartzler-says

Leder, M. (Producer), (2001). *Pay it forward [Motion Picture]*. United
    States: Warner Home Video. Retrieved from https://www.imdb.com/title/tt0223897/

Lopez, D., & Froese, T. M. (2016). Analysis of Costs and Benefits of
    Panelized and Modular Prefabricated Homes. *Science Direct.* Retrieved from
    https://www.sciencedirect.com/science/article/pii/S1877705816301734

Lounsberry, S. (2018). Planned Longmont tiny home village will give 25
    homeless veterans free temporary housing. *University Wire.* Retrieved from
    https://www.dailycamera.com/2018/11/03/planned-longmont-tiny-home-village-will-give-25-
    homeless-veterans-free-temporary-housing/

Mago, V. K., Morden, H. K., Fritz, C., Wu, T., Namazi, S., Geranmayeh,
    P., Chattopadhyay, R., & Dabbaghianp, V. (2013). Analyzing the impact of social factors on
    homelessness: a Fuzzy Cognitive Map approach. *National Center for Biotechnology Information*
    Company. Retrieved from https://www.ncbi.nlm.nih.gov/pmc/articles/PMC3766254/

MacKenzie, D., McNelis, S., Flatau, P., Valentine, K., & Seivwright A.
    (2017). The funding and delivery of programs to reduce homelessness: the case study evidence.
    Australian Housing and Urban Research Institute: Ahuri. Retrieved from
    https://www.ahuri.edu.au/research/final-reports/274

McCarty, D., Argeriou, M., Huebner, R. B., & Lubran, B. (1991).
    Alcoholism, drug abuse, and the homeless. *American Psychologist, 46(11), 1139-1148.*
    Retrieved from https://ohsu.pure.elsevier.com/en/publications/alcoholism-drug-abuse-and-the-
    homeless-2

McElroy, J. (2019). Vancouver's homeless count rises to highest number
    since survey began. *CBC News Company.* Retrieved from
    https://www.cbc.ca/news/canada/british-columbia/vancouver-homeless-count-2019-number-of-
    homeless-1.5172332

Merille, E. (2013). Florida International University Panther Statue.
    Retrieved from https://www.iflickr.com/photos/fiu/8489551367

Miami, FL Rental Market Trends. (2019). Average Rent in Miami and
    Rent Prices by Neighborhood. *RENTCafé Canada.* Retrieved from
    https://www.rentcafe.com/average-rent-market-trends/us/fl/miami/

Minnery, J., & Greenhalgh, E. (2007). Approaches to homelessness policy in Europe, the United States, and Australia. *Journal of Social Issues, 63*(3), 641-655. Retrieved from http://citeseerx.ist.psu.edu/viewdoc/download?doi=10.1.1.579.2521&rep=rep1&type=pdf

MintPress News Desk. (2015). Empty Homes Outnumber The Homeless 6 to 1, So Why Not Give Them Homes? *Mintpress News.* Retrieved from https://www.mintpressnews.com/empty-homes-outnumber-the-homeless-6-to-1-so-why-not-give-them-homes/207194/

Mitlin, D. (2007). Finance for low-income housing and community development. *International Institute for Environment and Development (IIED).* Retrieved from http://pubs.iied.org/pdfs/10557IIED.pdf

Montgomery, J. M. (Photographer). (2017, Circa January 2). Montgomery Family Crest [Digital Image].

Montgomery, J. M. (2019). *Homelessness Issues in Miami-Dade Florida.* Unpublished manuscript. Florida International University. Copyright 2019. Adapted with permission.

Montgomery, J. M. (2019). *Reducing Homelessness in Miami-Dade County.* Unpublished manuscript. Florida International University, Miami, FL. Copyright 2019. Adapted with permission.

Montgomery, M. & Alvarez, S. (2019). *Public Evaluation Design for Miami-Dade Home GAP.* Unpublished manuscript. Florida International University. Copyright 2019. Adapted with permission.

Montgomery, J. M. (2020). *A Solution to Reduce Homelessness in Miami-Dade and Abroad.* Unpublished manuscript. Florida International University, Miami, FL. Copyright 2020. Adapted with permission.

Montgomery, J. M. (Photographer). (2020, May 27). Montgomery Family Crest [Digital Image].

Moore, W.A. (2017, June 18). "Invisible Crisis: In Pinellas, the dearth of emergency shelters is a crisis for homeless families." *Tampa Bay Times*. Retrieved from https://www.tampabay.com/news/humaninterest/invisible-crisis-in-pinellas-dearth-of-emergency-shelters-is-a-crisis-for/2327475/

Moran, Joseph. (1997). Assessing Adult Learning. A Guide for
     Practitioners. Professional Practices in Adult Education and Human Resource Development
     Series. *Krieger Publishing Co.* Retrieved from https://eric.ed.gov/?id=ED401404

Mozloom, L. (2018). Miami-Dade County Homeless Trust reports
     homelessness in Miami-Dade is at a record low. *Miami-Dade County.* Retrieved from
     http://www.homelesstrust.org/releases/2018-02-12-homeless-census.asp

Mozloom, L. (2019, February 20). "Affordable housing critical to maintaining a downward trend of street
     homelessness in Miami-Dade County." *Miami-Made County*. Retrieved from
     http://www.homelesstrust.org/releases/2019-02-20-affordable-housing-critical.asp

Nelson, E. (2018). In the struggle to get its red-hot housing market
     under control, Vancouver targets Chinese buyers. *Quartz Media, Inc.* Retrieved from
     https://qz.com/1212136/vancouvers-speculation-tax-targets-chinese-property-investors-in-
     hopes-of-getting-its-housing-market-under-control/

Newcomer, K. E., Hatry, H. P., & Wholey, J. S. (2015). Handbook of
     Practical Program Evaluation, 4th Edition. *San Francisco, CA: John Wiley & Sons.* Retrieved from
     http://www.blancopeck.net/HandbookProgramEvaluation.pdf

Now this. (2018). Village of Tiny Homes Built for Homeless Veterans in
     Kansas City. *Now This News, A Group Nine Media Inc.* Retrieved from
     https://nowthisnews.com/videos/news/village-of-tiny-homes-built-for-homeless-veterans-in-
     kansas-city

Obama, B. (2016). Remarks at the Veterans Day Ceremony, Arlington,
     VA, November 11, 2016. The Obama Administration. Retrieved from
     https://obamawhitehouse.archives.gov/photos-and-video/video/2016/11/11/remarks-veterans-
     day-ceremony

Online Sunshine, (2019). The 2019 Florida Statutes, Chapter 1009,
     Educational Scholarships, Fees and Financial Assistance. Florida Legislature. Retrieved from
     http://www.leg.state.fl.us/statutes/index.cfm?App_mode=Display_Statute&URL=1000-
     1099/1009/Sections/1009.25.html

Operation Sacred Trust, (2019). Supportive Services for Veteran
     Families. *Purpose Built Families Foundation.* Retrieved from http://411veterans.com

Kantor, W. (2019). This Group's Village of Tiny Homes for Vets 'Saves
    Lives' While 'Setting Them Up for Success'. People.com Retrieved from
    https://people.com/human-interest/hero-group-veterans-community-project-tiny-homes/

Phillips, L. (2015). Homelessness: perception of causes and solutions.
    Journal of Poverty, 19(1), 1-19. Taylor & Francis Online. Retrieved from
    https://www.tandfonline.com/doi/abs/10.1080/10875549.2014.951981

Pi Alpha Alpha, (2020). The Global Honor Society for Public Affairs &
    Public Administration. Retrieved from http://pialphaalpha.org

Please, N. (2017). The Action Plan for Preventing Homelessness in
    Finland 2016-2019: The
    Culmination of an Integrated Strategy to End Homelessness? European Observatory on
    Homelessness. Retrieved from https://www.feantsaresearch.org/download/strategy-review-
    19029039682682325644.pdf

Poppe, B. (2015). The Path Forward: Rethinking Solutions for
    Homelessness in Florida. Florida Department of Children and Families. Retrieved from
    https://www.cfch.org/wp-content/uploads/2018/04/Path-Forward-Final-LONG-LO-RES-9-16-
    15.pdf

Richardson, B. (2019). America's Housing Affordability Crisis Only
    Getting Worse. Forbes Media LLC. Retrieved from
    https://www.forbes.com/sites/brendarichardson/2019/01/31/americas-housing-affordability-
    crisis-only-getting-worse/#679048d4104b

Rojc, P. (2017). A Bank Looks to Move the Needle on Affordable
    Housing. Inside Philanthropy. Retrieved from
    https://www.insidephilanthropy.com/home/2017/6/6/can-a-bank-move-the-needle-on-
    affordable-housing

Rusty Eric, Quotes. (n.d.). The Fighter Within. The Greed Philosophy. Blogspot.com Retrieved April 24,
    2020. From https://leavingfootprintsonthesandsoftime.blogspot.com/2014/04/the-greed-
    philosophy.html

Sacred Heart Mission. (2019). Why our program Journey to Social
    Inclusion (J2SI) really works. Sacred Heart Mission. Retrieved from
    https://www.sacredheartmission.org/news-media/our-blog/why-our-program-journey-to-social-
    inclusion-j2si-really-works

Semuels, A. (2018). How Can the U.S. End Homelessness? *The Atlantic.*
Retrieved from https://www.theatlantic.com/business/archive/2016/04/end-homelessness-us/479115/

Schwartz, A. F. (2018). Strategies for Improving Homeless People's
Access to Mainstream Benefits and Services. HUD USER. (2010). *huduser.gov.* Retrieved from
https://www.huduser.gov/portal/publications/povsoc/homeless_access.html

The World Bank. (2016). *Ending Extreme Poverty. The World Bank,*
IBRD-IDA. Retrieved
from https://www.worldbank.org/en/news/feature/2016/06/08/ending-extreme-poverty

Toepfer, K. (2000). Strategies to combat homelessness. *United Nations
Human Centre for Human Settlements (Habitat).* Retrieved from
http://mirror.unhabitat.org/documents/HS-599x.pdf

Treglia, D., Watts, B., & Pomeroy, J. (2013). A Literature Review on
Approaches to End Family Homelessness. *Focus Consulting, Inc.* Retrieved from
http://www.focus-consult.com/wp-content/uploads/Literature_Review-on-Family-Homelessness-May-2013.pdf

Tsai, J., & Wilson, M. (2020). COVID-19: A potential public health problem for homeless
populations. *The Lancet Public Health, 5*(4). Retrieved from
https://www.thelancet.com/journals/lanpub/article/PIIS2468-2667(20)30053-0/fulltext

Turner, A. (2019). Bringing it All Together: Integrating Services to
Address Homelessness. *SSRN.* Retrieved from
https://papers.ssrn.com/sol3/papers.cfm?abstract_id=3313701

Ullman, M. D. (2016). STATE OF FLORIDA REPORT: 2016 Homeless
Census Estimates and
Funding Need to End Chronic Homelessness. *National Homeless Information Project.* Retrieved
from
https://www.nhipdata.org/local/upload/file/Florida%20Homeless%20Report%202016%20%2009_30_16%20-%20final%20report.pdf

United Nations. (2019). Transforming our world: the 2030 Agenda for
Sustainable Development. Sustainable Development Goals Knowledge Platform. *United Nations.*
Retrieved from https://sustainabledevelopment.un.org/post2015/transformingourworld

Utržan, D. S., Piehler, T. F., Gewirtz, A. H., & August, G. J. (2017).
Stressful life events and perceived parental control in formerly homeless families: Impact on child-internalizing symptoms. American Journal of Orthopsychiatry, 87(3), 317. *US National Library of Medicine National Institutes of Health.* Retrieved from https://www.ncbi.nlm.nih.gov/pmc/articles/PMC5647151/

VHA Office of Mental Health. (2012). Homeless Veterans. U.S.
Department of Housing and Urban Development-VA Supportive Housing (HUD-VASH) Program. *Veterans Administration.* Retrieved from https://www.va.gov/homeless/hud-vash.asp

Wheelock, D. C. (2006). What Happens to Banks When House Prices
Fall? U.S. Regional Housing Busts of the 1980s and 1990s. The Federal Reserve Bank of St. Louis. Retrieved from https://files.stlouisfed.org/files/htdocs/publications/review/06/09/Wheelock.pdf

Wiggins, S. (2007). Rural employment and migration: In search of
decent work. ODI, Overseas Development Institute. *Federal Reserve Bank of St. Louis.* Retrieved from https://www.odi.org/publications/5-rural-employment-and-migration-search-decent-work

Winch, P., Shen, Q., & Schwartz, A. (2011). Low-Income Housing Tax
Credit Developments and Neighborhood Change: A Case Study of Miami-Dade County. *Taylor & Francis Online.* Retrieved from https://www.tandfonline.com/doi/abs/10.1080/02673037.2011.593130

Wright, J. (2017). Poor and homeless in the sunshine state: Down and
out in theme park nation. *Routledge.* Retrieved from https://sites.google.com/site/clickdownloadpdf5/download-pdf-books-poor-and-homeless-in-the-sunshine-state-down-and-out-in-theme-park-nation-read-online-by-james-wright

Zufferey, C. (2016). Homelessness and social work: An intersectional
approach. *Routledge.* Retrieved from https://www.feantsaresearch.org/download/feantsa-ejh-11-1_br1-v036322666244600554715.pdf

Appendix A – Cost-Benefit Analysis Data Sheet

Chart 14 – Cost-Benefit Analysis Data Sheet[128]

A: Do Nothing.			
Do Nothing.		**Y0**	**Y1**
Costs - of dealing with homeless in Miami.	S	44,678,282.00 S	44,678,282.00
Benefits - From Banks Paying Property Tax.	S	1,228,480.00 S	1,228,480.00
Discount Rate		0	5%
Discount Factor		0	0.9346
Discounted Benefits =			S 1,228,480.00
Discounted Costs =			S 44,678,282.00
		+	S 44,678,282.00
		+	S 44,678,282.00
Net Present Value (NPV) =			S (178,152,878.16)
Benefit Cost Ratio (BCR) =			0.027496133

	S (6,982,800.00)	Reduction Each Year. S	12,212,200.00
B: Build individual homes on donated land.	S	25,000.00	Per Home time 3,839 =
Build 600 Homes each year.		**Y0**	**Y1**
Costs of dealing with homeless in Miami plus building homes.	S	44,678,282.00 S	46,001,969.20
Benefits - Property Tax Revenue from building homes for homeless.	S	-	$245,696
Discount Rate		0	5%
Discount Factor		0	0.9346
Discounted Benefits =			S 245,696.00
Discounted Costs =			S 46,001,969.20
		+	S 28,130,656.40
		+	S 10,259,343.60
Net Present Value (NPV) =			S (117,402,823.98)
Benefit Cost Ratio (BCR) =			0.023993604

C: Non-Income Producing - Receive Tax Breaks.		Reduction Each Year. S	(8,935,656.40)
Bank Home Giveaways - 3,000 Homes Gifted -Give 600 Homes each year.		**Y0**	**Y1**
Costs	S	44,678,282.00 S	35,742,625.60
Benefits	S	-	$245,696
Discount Rate		0	5%
Discount Factor		0	0.9346
Discounted Benefits =			S 245,696.00
Discounted Costs =			S 35,742,625.60
		+	S 17,871,312.80
		+	S 0.00
Net Present Value (NPV) =			S (75,337,463.35)
Benefit Cost Ratio (BCR) =			0.036896349

Cost-Benefit Analysis Data Sheet (Montgomery, 2019).

[128] M. Montgomery. "Reducing Homelessness in Miami." Unpublished manuscript. *Florida International University.* (Copyright, 2019).

Appendix A – Cost-Benefit Analysis Data Sheet

Chart 15 – Cost-Benefit Analysis Data Sheet[129]

	Y2		Y3		Y4		Y5		Costs
$	44,678,282.00	$	44,678,282.00	$	44,678,282.00	$	44,678,282.00	$	(268,069,692.00)
$	1,228,480.00	$	1,228,480.00	$	1,228,480.00	$	1,228,480.00	$	7,370,880.00
	5%		5%		5%		5%		
	0.8734		0.8163		0.7629		0.713		
								$	(260,698,812.00)
	0.9346		=	$	5,037,013.70				Deficit plus Profit
	0.9346	+		$	44,678,282.00		0.8734		
	0.8163	+		$	44,678,282.00		0.7629		
	0.713	–		$	183,189,891.86				

(NVP)

(BCR)

	Y2		Y3		Y4		Y5		
$	12,212,200.00	$	12,212,200.00	$	12,212,200.00	$	12,212,200.00	$	(61,061,000.00)
$	95,975,000.00	Property Tax Revenue -	$320*3839 = $1,228,480		$320 per home =		$	1,228,480.00	
	Y2		Y3		Y4		Y5		Costs
$	37,066,312.80	$	28,130,656.40	$	19,195,000.00	$	10,259,343.60	$	(185,331,564.00)
	$491,392		$737,088		$982,784		$1,228,480		$1,228,480
	5%		5%		5%		5%	$	3,685,440.00
	0.8734		0.8163		0.7629		0.713		
								$	19,195,000.00
	0.9346		=	$	2,886,166.34				Each year for homes.
	0.9346	+		$	37,066,312.80		0.8734	$	(200,841,124.00)
	0.8163	+		$	19,195,000.00		0.7629		Deficit plus Profit
	0.713	–		$	120,288,990.32				Costs of building homes / 5 Years
								$	(8,935,656.40)

(NVP)

| | | | | | | | | $ | 10,259,343.60 |

(BCR)

	Y2		Y3		Y4		Y5		
$	(8,935,656.40)	$	(8,935,656.40)	$	(8,935,656.40)	$	(8,935,656.40)	$	(44,678,282.00)
	Y2		Y3		Y4		Y5		Costs
$	26,806,969.20	$	17,871,312.80	$	8,935,656.40	$	0.00	$	-
	$491,392		$737,088		$982,784		$1,228,480	$	3,685,440.00
	5%		5%		5%		5%		
	0.8734		0.8163		0.7629		0.713	$	48,363,722.00
									Profiting
	0.9346		=	$	2,886,166.34				
								$	48,363,722.00
	0.9346	+		$	26,806,969.20		0.8734		Savings plus Profit
	0.8163	+		$	8,935,656.40		0.7629		
	0.713	=		$	78,223,629.69				

(NVP)

(BCR)

Cost-Benefit Analysis Data Sheet (Montgomery, 2019).

---

[129] M. Montgomery. "Reducing Homelessness in Miami." Unpublished manuscript. *Florida International University.* (Copyright, 2019).

Appendix B – Participant Survey Questionnaire

Participant Data Collection / Survey[130]

Home GAP Participant Survey

Homeless participants in the Home GAP Initiative is Miami-Dade's number one priority in achieving the goal of ZERO homelessness within the county borders. Please fill out the survey below to help us make the necessary improvements towards developing a continually better program for future participants.

1 - Strongly Disagree / 2 - Disagree / 3 – Somewhat Disagree
4 – Neutral
5 – Somewhat Agree / 6 – Agree / 7 - Strongly Disagree

Chart 16 – Participant Survey Questionnaire

	1	2	3	4	5	6	7
1. I believe that my assigned social worker was attentive in helping design my treatment plan.							
2. I was treated with respect throughout the Home GAP Initiative.							
3. I believe that Miami-Dade County officials had my best interests at heart.							
4. I believe the Home GAP is the best option for homeless individuals.							

5. I was treated fairly throughout the program.						
6. I felt no pressure to participate in my treatment plan.						
7. Mental health professionals helped meet my personal needs.						
8. I would recommend this program intervention to others.						
9. Participation in group therapy for my treatment plan was well organized and met my specific needs.						
10. Each stage of the Home GAP Initiative was clearly explained to me.						
11. Adequate time was given to me to prepare for each stage of my treatment plan.						
12. Achieving goals in my treatment plan was an essential part of achieving the result of the Home GAP.						

13. Having a sponsor and a therapist for my treatment plan was important to me.						
14. I feel good about my future now that I have graduated from the Home GAP.						

Participant Survey Questionnaire (Montgomery & Alvarez, 2019).

1. What would you change to make the program better?

(Please write your response below).

Appendix C – Employee Survey Questionnaire

Employee Data Collection / Survey [131]

Home GAP Employee Survey

Homeless Employees in the Home GAP Initiative is Miami-Dade's number one priority in achieving the goal of ZERO homelessness within the county borders. Please fill out the survey below to help us make the necessary improvements towards developing a continually better program for future employees.

1 - Strongly Disagree / 2 - Disagree / 3 – Somewhat Disagree
4 – Neutral
5 – Somewhat Agree / 6 – Agree / 7 - Strongly Disagree

Chart 17 – Employee Survey Questionnaire

	1	2	3	4	5	6	7
1. I think the Home GAP Initiative is useful for homeless individuals.							
2. I believe that management listened to any of my suggestions about changes that needed to occur.							
3. I believe that the Home GAP Initiative teams worked well with one another.							
4. I see myself still working in the Home GAP Initiative in two years.							
5. I believe that the leadership communicated their vision and ideas that motivated me.							
6. I believe that I had all the necessary tools to do my job effectively.							
7. Day-to-Day decisions by team members were in the interest of the client.							

---

[131] Copyright Statement - From "Public Evaluation Design for Miami-Dade Home GAP," by J. Michael Montgomery and Sandro Alvarez, 2019: Unpublished manuscript. *Florida International University.* Adapted with permission.

8. I knew what my obligations were to be successful in my role as a helper within the Home GAP Initiative.						
9. My coworkers have the experience and skillsets to do their jobs well.						
10. I felt safe when working with clients in the Home GAP Initiative Program.						
11. I feel comfortable sharing my opinion with others during an "All-Hands" team meeting.						
12. I feel that I belong to the Home GAP Initiative Team.						
13. I received the appropriate recognition for the work I did.						
14. I am proud to be working for the Home GAP Initiative.						

Employee Survey Questionnaire (Montgomery & Alvarez, 2019).

1. What would you change to make the program better?

(Please write your response below).

**"Always remember,
your focus determines your reality."**

[132]George Lucas – Film Maker

---

[132] From "Quotes.net" by George Lucas Filmmaker. (n.d.)

NOTES

NOTES

NOTES

NOTES

NOTES

NOTES

NOTES

NOTES

NOTES

Figure 6. Montgomery, J. M. (Photographer, 2017).

Thanks for Reading!
I hope that together we can make a difference
to "End Homelessness Now!"

J. M. Montgomery
Active Member of:

The National Society of Leadership and Success.
Sigma Alpha Pi – Σ A Π – Honor Society
Executive Leadership Certified
http://www.nsls.org

My goal for the future is to simply find a federal job so that I can retire with my
federal pension after nine more years of employment.
Maybe I can work for you?

$39.95
ISBN 978-1-7351324-3-3
53995>

9 781735 132433

CPSIA information can be obtained
at www.ICGtesting.com
Printed in the USA
BVHW010813200620
581884BV00003B/15